THE ROMAN ROAD REVISITED

NEW VISTAS ON THE ROAD TO RESURRECTION LIVING

Books By Steve Elkins

*A Living Soul: Ethical Implications of Technologically
    Assisted Reproduction*
A Short Course in Spiritual Leadership
Understanding the Gospel
Current Issues Concerning Lordship Salvation
Forgotten Fundamentals of the Swing
Pitch Like the Pro's

THE ROMAN ROAD REVISITED

NEW VISTAS ON THE ROAD TO RESURRECTION LIVING

Steve Elkins

Allie Grace Books

Dallas, Texas

The Roman Road Revisited

Copyright © 2005

Published by Allie Grace Books
A division of Allie Grace Publishers
9706 La Prada
Dallas, Texas 75228

Cover Design: Master's Press   Cover photo: Pashnit.com

First printing, 2005

Printed in the United States of America

Elkins, Stephen, 1956-
   The Roman Road Revisited: New Vistas on the Road to Resurrection Living/ Steve Elkins

ISBN 0-9765470-0-7

Edited by Michael D. Makidon

TO

Marci for her encouragement, wisdom and grace. . .

Zane Hodges, mentor and dear friend. . .

And to our wonderful Young Life family in East Dallas, kids,
leaders and committee. . .

*Yet in all these things we are more than conquerors through Him who
loved us. . .*

CONTENTS

CONTENTS

Section III   *Much More Good News: Victory!*
Romans 5:1–8:39

Section IV   *Good News: Summary*
Romans 9–16

Introduction

I have a tri-athlete friend who just ran his first White Rock marathon. He ran hard and did better than expected, but was terribly disappointed at the finish. All the other races and events he'd been in had wonderful freebies and festive atmospheres at the end. Contestants were treated like royalty—food, drinks, free items of all kinds, live bands and that kind of thing. But at this one, besides announcing his name, all he got was a Coke, a medal, and a little fruit... *and that was it!*

"This is really lousy!" he thought to himself. All the way home he was ticked. "I gave it my best effort, a *national* race, and that's *all we get?!*" He couldn't believe it. What a disappointment.

As he went through the front door, still steaming because of the shoddy conclusion, he collapsed in his chair and thumbed through the race packet.

What a fool he felt like when he discovered that all the hoopla, the post-race contestants' celebration, was to take place *in* the building. The American Airlines Center was full of gifts, freebies, live bands, free massages, drink, food and partying through the afternoon and into the night! ...Now it was too late. He had missed it all, and all because he hadn't read the packet!

That sounds like a lot of people I know. An inner frustration gnaws at them. A feeling that there is something more to life than they are experiencing. They're not exactly sure what it is or how to get there, but in their gut they're sure of this: there's something more and they're missing out.

It's quite likely they *are* missing out. As we'll see, even Christians who possess eternal life far too often are *experiencing* "death." Their existence is far short of the supernatural, resurrection life of peace, joy, love and victory described in Romans and available to every believer right now.

Like my friend, you might have glanced at the "packet," but not looked carefully at its contents. If so, we invite you to take another look at the life-giving message of Romans. Let's look at it carefully. You might have gone down this Romans Road many times. But this time, I believe with all my heart, if you'll have open eyes you're going to see some things on this trip you've never seen before.

Unlike my disillusioned friend, who felt after his race, "Is this all there is?" my prayer is that after this book you'll have the real and heartfelt sensation, "I never dreamt it was meant to be this good!"

Preview

The thematic statement for the book of Romans is at its beginning, "For I am not ashamed of the gospel of Christ, for it is the power of God to salvation for everyone who believes, for the Jew first and also for the Greek. For in it the righteousness of God is revealed from faith to faith; as it is written, 'The just shall live by faith'" (1:16-17).

A Powerful Gospel

This *gospel* "good news" of Christ is about *God's* dynamite *"power"* (*dunamis*)—not ours. The same kind of spiritual *power* the Holy Spirit used to raise Christ from the dead (1:4) is the same kind of spiritual power that will give us new life, too (8:13), and by which He can cause us to be filled "with all joy and peace in believing that we may abound in hope by the *power* of the Holy Spirit" (15:13). This is supernatural, *spiritual power!*

The gospel of Romans is about God's power *to salvation*. As we'll see, this "gospel" and "salvation" is broader than how we commonly use the terms. It is not just the "gospel" of how to get eternal life. It is not just the "salvation" which delivers from hell. Repeatedly he says, this *salvation* is *"much more"* than just that (see Romans 5:9-10).

Much More Than Just Salvation From Hell

To be exact, the *gospel* and *salvation* Paul concerns himself with in Romans is about being saved from God's *present wrath*— which includes how to get eternal life and how to be "saved" from hell, but it is *much more* than just that.

In these modern times we don't like to think of a God who has wrath. One modern "theologian" has said, "The God of the Old Testament (One who could be angry or wrathful) does not exist anymore." Paul paints quite a different picture. Then he describes in detail the terms for escaping God's present wrath.

Based On A Faith Principle

The summary heading continues, ''For in it (the gospel) the righteousness of God is revealed from faith to faith; as it is written, 'The just shall live by faith''' (1:17). Not only does this gospel reveal the *righteousness* God gives as a gift to everyone who *believes* (4:5-6), but he also has in mind the everyday kind of righteousness that should become part of our experience (8:4). Our "positional" righteousness before God is by faith (*justification,* chapters 4 and 5). Our "practical" righteousness before men is also by faith (*sanctification* chapters 6 through 8). "From *faith* to *faith*," the Christian life is characterized by faith from start to finish. Not only do we receive the gift of eternal life by the one simple act of faith, we are enabled to *experience* that life—true life filled with joy and peace and hope—as we walk in faith.

Possessing Eternal Life Vs. Experiencing It

Perhaps you have already experienced that there is a big difference between merely *possessing* eternal life (1:18–5:10), and *experiencing* the eternal life you possess (5:10ff.)! Paul did as well, and he will share with us the personal victory he won through this powerful, life-giving gospel.

Gary Brandenburg has used a simple outline for teaching through Romans in four weeks. He looks at the four "Therefore's" of Romans 2:1, 5:1, 8:1 and 12:1. Those "therefore" verses trace the overall movements of the book. Though this isn't an outline of Romans *per se*, we are going to take a look at the themes Paul surfaces in Romans. Furthermore, Lord willing, we will look at a key that absolutely unlocks the book and makes it come alive with all the power the Lord intended. It will be the *Roman Road Revisited,* and you're in for some new destinations!

———

Each section has seven readings intended to take fifteen minutes or so daily. If you look up some of the passages or endnotes it might take a little more time than that. We hope the book is reader friendly and motivates you to study the Bible more seriously on your own.

At the back are simple overview Bible studies covering the chapters of Romans according to our sections. In other words, there is an overview study for Section I (Romans 1:1–3:20), Section II (Romans 3:21–4:25), and so forth, all found in the back of the book, just before the endnotes. In addition to reading beforehand the portion of Scripture that applies to these sections, you might want to avail yourself of these overview studies. They can assist your Bible reading and make it more enjoyable and beneficial.

In the process of learning about the power for resurrection life here and now, we hope you'll appreciate more clearly than ever the simple, beautiful terms of the gospel of grace. It is our prayer that as a result you'll love the Savior more and increasingly appreciate what He has done—*and does*—to make this gospel so wonderful.

SE

Section I

Romans 1:1–3:20

Bad News: Judgment

"Therefore you are without excuse,
every man of you who passes judgment,
for in that you judge another,
you condemn yourself;
for you who judge practice the same things.
And we know that the judgment of God
rightly falls
upon those who practice such things."

Romans 2:1-2

1

God's Wrath
(Suggested Reading, Romans 1)

> *"For the wrath of God is revealed from heaven*
> *against all ungodliness and unrighteousness of men,*
> *who suppress the truth in unrighteousness."*
> Romans 1:18

Have you ever had a stubborn fourteen year old son? I have a great relationship with mine, *most of the time*... I couldn't have designed a neater kid. Fortunately he does great with his friends, teachers, coaches... but sometimes, *whew*, we butt heads!

Like at the batting cage last night (we take our hitting seriously). I wanted him just a little closer to the plate. What did he do? Intentionally got way *too* close. . . or he didn't move at all. . . or he'd move closer like I wanted, but purposefully not give a good effort on the swing. Anything and everything but my simple request! He was out to prove, by golly, "I know better than dad. I'm going to do it my way." I only wanted him to *try* something, give it an honest effort. The more I talked, the more he mocked... and the more my blood boiled. We know how to push each other's buttons!

Wrath. Anger. Not the words we like to associate with God. Of course, we know He did some very strong things in the

Old Testament, but Jesus, who is God in flesh and who came to "explain" God to us, did get angry at times. Nevertheless we tend to think of Him as a kinder, gentler version of the "wrathful" God of the Old Testament. But why would we think God has changed? Paul reminds us in Romans 1:18-32 that He hasn't. A quick overview of those verses will tell us some insightful things about God's wrath.

God's wrath is *timeless.* It "*is* revealed from heaven against all ungodliness and unrighteousness..." Whether in the old days or the new, God's wrath is still present. Embedded in the illustration that follows, verses 19-32, is an example of how God's *present wrath* operates here and now. (Interestingly, Paul is fond of speaking of God's *temporal* wrath more than His *eternal* wrath).

God's wrath is *universal.* It is against "*all* unrighteousness and ungodliness of men..." Not only is it against all sins, big and small, it is impartial to mankind. Whether rich or poor, white or black, "Jew or Gentile," it is universal.

God's wrath *fits the crime.* Paul pictures God's present-tense wrath with a case of people who have dishonored God. The punishment? God dishonors them. The interesting thing is how He does it.

Sometimes, Paul explains, God's wrath is seen in the natural unfolding of the sin itself. In other words, He gives us freedom to do things He does not want—things He knows are not proper and not best. Along with that freedom is the inherent danger of reaping the consequences of unrighteous, ungodly choices. It is hard not to notice the "tough love" of verses 24, 26 and 28, *"God gave them over... God gave them over... God gave them over."* Giving them over to their sins of (free) choice, includes giving them over to the working out of the natural consequences of those choices. That's how God's wrath can work itself out, then and now. The "present tenseness" of His wrath is embedded throughout the illustration and nowhere more vividly than, *"receiving* in their own persons the due penalty of their error" (1:27). Note: the "receiving" of the penalty is present tense; not "They *will* receive...," but are receiving *presently.*

Suppressing the truth about God in unrighteousness pushes God's buttons. Our question should be, how can we escape such wrath? The good news of Romans is the answer.

Personal Reflection:

1. Concerning this idea of God being wrathful, does it bother you? If so why?

2. Can you think of a time, or times, in your life when God "gave you over" to the punishing consequences of your bad choices?

Further Thoughts:

"Why is God angry?" you might ask. First, it should go without saying that His anger is not always like ours. Ours is too often from wrong reasons, at the wrong time, in the wrong measure, directed at the wrong object, etc. We get "mad" when we're angry, as if we lose rationality. Like going crazy at the driver who cut us off. God doesn't get "mad" like that. His anger is perfectly justified, measured and actually loving.

For instance, you probably don't have problems with the fact that God is also a "jealous" God (Ex 20:5). Not in a sinful way, but out of His love. He knows and wants what is best for us. Just as you are jealous, in a good way, for your kids that their affections are not misplaced on those things that could do them great harm, God is as well. James says to us who have become too friendly with the world, departing from God, "The Spirit whom He has made to dwell in us (God's Spirit) *longs jealously* over us" (Jas 4:5). Hopefully we understand His jealousy in terms of His perfect tender love for us. We shouldn't see His anger any differently.

I know of a lady who divorced her husband partly because she thought *any show* of anger was wrong. Her father was extremely passive and she was trying to "castrate" her husband's normal, healthy, male anger—the kind of healthy male anger that Dr. Laura and other counselors have said is a necessary ingredient for raising kids, especially boys. Do we try to "castrate" God? Make a kinder, gentler version? He is what He is. Let's find out what He is really like, and not just what we think He is like.

Why is He angry? Out of love. If you're a child of God it's only for your good. It's what you need, in just the right measure. Though painful, it is exercised to yield the "peaceable fruit of righteousness" in us (Heb 12:5-11). If you're not a child of God, it is intended as part of His kindness to lead you to repentance and ultimately to faith in Christ. His wrath is with the intention of blessing.

His anger is not capricious. It is against those who "suppress the truth" of God in unrighteousness. That's a big deal. Suppressing God's truth can have eternal ramifications, not to mention disastrous ones here and now! His anger is our choice. It is our actions that rouse Him.

God has provided a means of deliverance from His present and future wrath. Persevere through this first section on "Bad News: Judgment" as it is important to realizing just how desperately we need to be delivered.

The more we apprehend the bleakness of the bad news, the more we'll appreciate the beauty of the good news to come.

Group Questions:

1. Have you ever had a time when you were angry in a "good" way?

2. Does thinking of God as expressing anger disturb you? Why or why not?

3. What if God's wrath weren't there? What attitude would you prefer He had toward sin?

4. Explain how God's wrath is displayed through the natural consequences of sin.

Judgment
(Suggested Reading, Romans 2)

> *"Therefore you are without excuse,*
> *every man of you who passes judgment,*
> *for in that you judge another, you condemn yourself;*
> *for you who judge practice the same things.*
> *And we know that the judgment of God rightly falls*
> *upon those who practice such things."*
> Romans 2:1-2

We get tickets to the Mesquite Rodeo about once a year. What a hoot. Pure entertainment. They know how to put on a show—I get mesmerized just watching the tractor re-plow the arena. One of the most exciting events is the calf-roping. What skill! Chasing a calf at break-neck speed, lassoing him in, jumping off, wrestling him down, tying him up... in a matter of blinks.

Right now, we are the calf and Paul is the roper. He throws an accurate lariat, right around our necks. All that remains is tightening the noose. There is no escaping.

Paul offers an ingenious self-evident proof that we are all sinners deserving of God's wrath. He appeals to a favorite universal past-time, *judging others*. We all do it, don't we? Judging others is proof that we have an inherent moral code within us (otherwise why would we have been judging?). If we're honest, we would each have to admit that we have broken this universal internal moral code. Paul knows he's got us. We're without excuse, for the very things we have judged others we have done ourselves! There's no wiggle room, "for you who judge practice the same things."

We've condemned ourselves. And what's worse, God condemns us too. "And we know that the *judgment of God* is according to truth against those who practice such things." Later we'll see how to live a life free from such condemnation. But Paul is not ready to go there just yet.

Do you remember the *wrath* we talked about in the last chapter? Here it is again, but instead of present wrath, it's future wrath. "Because of your stubbornness and unrepentant heart you are storing up *wrath* for yourself in the *day of wrath* and revelation of the righteous judgment of God, who 'will render to every man according to his deeds'" (2:5-6).

Lest you think you might slip out of the noose, he repeats,

> For we have already charged that both Jews
> and Greeks are all under sin; as it is written,
> "There is none righteous, no, not one;
> There is none who understands; There is none
> who seeks after God; They have all turned aside;
> They have together become unprofitable;
> There is none who does good, no, not one..."
> Romans 3:9-12

"No, not one" of us escapes the noose of sin. Paul uses these Old Testament verses to prove to his fellow Jews that they

and "*all the world* are guilty before God" (1:21). He's a lassoing expert with the lariat of God's Word, and we can't wiggle loose.

Personal Reflection:

1. What are some things you've judged others of that you are guilty of yourself?

2. Read Romans 2:2, 5-6. How do the thoughts of "judgment" and "wrath" make you feel?

Further Thoughts:

What is something that "drives you crazy" in others? Something irritating which others do? "Road Rage" is popular. Several times I've been in a car driven by a sweet Christian person. Someone pulls in front of him, or isn't driving well, and my Christian friend morphs suddenly into a Jekyll and Hyde kind of thing. (To this point in my life, the driving of others hasn't bothered me. Except my wife's, but that's another story. I'm such a bad driver, perhaps I know I can't be throwing stones. I need all the mercy I can get! But this doesn't excuse me from the point about to be made. Fact is, there are *other things* that unduly irritate *me*, but might not somebody else!)

Regardless of what it is, we all have things about others that put a burr under our saddles.

People who get upset at others' driving could probably pinpoint the irritant. Carelessness. Rudeness. Selfishness. Whatever it is that bothers these drivers, mark it down: They are guilty of the same thing! *"You who judge practice the same things"* (2:1-2). Don't misunderstand. The person judging the other drivers might be a *meticulous* motorist himself. But the specific character flaw that so ruffles his feathers—the carelessness, laziness, selfishness, dangerousness… whatever it is—he is guilty of it himself. Perhaps expressed in a completely different venue, but we are guilty of what we judge others. We'd admit it, too, if we were honest.

Group Questions:

1. What really upsets you in others?

2. Why is "judging" others evidence of an internal moral code?

3. How do "we" know that the "judgment of God rightly falls upon those who practice such things?"

4. Passing judgment on others happens first in our heart, then we might or might not make it public. Have you ever known anyone who didn't make judgments *in their heart* on people's actions or character?

5. In I Corinthians 4–5 Paul says we are to judge actions, but not motives—only God ultimately knows one's heart. Why would it be unhealthy (or unsafe) *not to judge actions* and the character they reveal?

3

Universal Standard

"who show the work of the law written in their hearts,
their conscience also bearing witness,
and between themselves their thoughts accusing or else excusing them"
Romans 2:15

"We hold these truths to be self-evident..." A self-evident truth is something that needs no proof or argument. Paul is nothing if not a lawyer. He builds his case against us with self-evident truth. Perry Mason couldn't find a hole in this argument. The result? We'll have to listen quietly to the verdict.

It is self-evident that there is a universal moral law, a standard, to which we are all subject. Even for the totally non-religious person, or the tribe farthest removed from civilization, we experience this law *"written in our hearts"* every time our conscience is at work. Every time we quarrel we're appealing to the fact that there is a universally accepted standard. Every time we sense the feeling of rightness and wrongness it is testimony to that standard. Every time you hear a teenager declare, "It's just not fair!," you've seen witness to this universal internal moral code.

Even atheists have these feelings! The nihilist, who says life is meaningless and that there are no absolutes, lives his life practically in such a way that shows he intuitively knows we are subject to universal laws (and he expects others to keep them, at least when he might be the one to be wronged!).

The verse above is in reference to the "Gentiles, who do not have the law," (v. 14) as opposed to the Jews who have God's written Laws. He says they instinctively—by nature—"do the things in the law," and "although not having the law are a law to themselves." This doesn't at all mean that they *always* "do the things of the law," only that they attempt to and expect others to do so. In fact this is Paul's very point: No one fully keeps the general moral standard that God has placed within every man. "For as many as have sinned without the law will also perish without the law, and as many as have sinned under the law will be judged by the law; for not the hearers of the law are justified before God, but the doers of the law will be justified" (2:12-13).

Yes, the *"doers of the law will be justified,"* but that's the rub. No one in history, outside of the Lord Jesus Christ, will ever be a "doer" of the law... not to the degree of deserving right standing before the righteous counsel of God. Paul will get to this shortly when he says, "For by the works of the law shall *no flesh* be justified before Him" (3:20).

Paul painstakingly demonstrates throughout chapter two and the first half of three, that whether one is a Gentile without the law, or a Jew with the law, all are under the verdict of being sinners, lawbreakers. Like a great lawyer he masterfully builds his case for the good news to come, "that every mouth may be stopped and *all the world* may become guilty before God" (3:19). His arguments show cause for us to listen carefully. If we're wise, we'll rest our case.

Have you seen lawyers and politicians debate on *Nightline*? They talk over each other, not giving the other a chance. Often what good points might have been made are never heard. With self-evident, inescapable arguments Paul is winning the right to have us listen carefully to his conclusions. Conclusions that have to be accepted by faith. Conclusions that are the difference between life and death. The more quietly we accept our guilt, the greater the music of the good news will be to our ears.

Personal Reflection:

1. When was the last time you went against your conscience?

2. Reflect on how you have seen this universal moral standard in play, whether acknowledged or not.

Further Thoughts:

There are many "self-evident" truths which need no argument. That "I exist" is self-evident in that I have to exist to think I don't exist! That "truth" exists is self-evident, since one cannot meaningfully deny truth without making a "truth statement" to the effect that there is no truth (*or that one cannot make "truth statements!"*)

That we have a conscience, "laws written in our hearts," with thoughts that *ac*cuse or *ex*cuse, is a universal, "self-evident," phenomenon. We have all done things that caused us to have the pangs of guilt, or a guilty conscience. We have all had the inner thoughts of duty or "ought-ness."

That a conscience can be educated and conditioned implies its existence prior to those things. For instance a screaming, crying baby does not need to be taught the terrifying emotion of being left. That is an unlearned universal reality. Until learning otherwise (that mommy will come back momentarily), healthy babies cry when they feel insecure. Babies feel and express emotional pain before they know what emotional pain is or what causes it. It's not learned. That our consciences also pre-date conditioning is seen in the fact that we often feel guilty over things we wish we didn't have to feel guilty about! We're like Lady Macbeth, washing her hands and crying continually, "Out damned spot, out," all to no effect. That there are divinely written laws on our heart is something to which our conscience bears witness every time we feel guilty.

Group Questions:

1. Why do you suppose this is a universal phenomena, that everyone goes against his conscience?

2. How is the universal feeling of rightness and wrongness—which crosses all religious/ non-religious lines, ethnicities and demographics—testimony to *"the law written in our hearts"*?

3. What could you draw from the fact that none of us always act the way we expect others to?

4. Someone once said, "An unregenerate heart makes a poor writing tablet for God." What might he have meant?

Rationalization

(Suggested Reading, Romans 3)

> *"And why not say, 'Let us do evil that good may come'?—*
> *as we are slanderously reported and as some affirm that we say.*
> *Their condemnation is just."*
> Romans 3:8

Have you ever rationalized your sin? Tried to justify it? Played the mind games to explain it away? If you have trouble thinking of times where you have, believe me, I've done enough for both of us. Why am I finding pleasure in realizing I'm not the only one who has played this game?

It's been going on since the beginning. Adam blamed it on the woman, "It's *her* fault" (that I disobeyed and am now afraid, naked, ashamed, and hiding). But when he added, the woman "whom *You gave* to be with me. . ." he was also *blaming God*. The woman did as much when she blamed it on the devil, "The *serpent* deceived me. . ."

The setting, characters and the wording may change, but the plot remains the same. We are constantly trying to rationalize our sin. Whether one believes in God or not, the guilt and shame of sin is scripted in our souls. If we don't repent and look to God for His cure, we'll grasp for whichever rationalization is convenient no matter how ridiculous.

Paul alludes to this in 3:5-8.[1] Verse 5 is an example of man employing whatever argument possible to get around the justness of God's wrath, to the conclusion that God is "unjust to inflict wrath." This is the trend of liberal psychology. What once was called sinful, became a "sickness." Later, what was "sickness" became "alternative lifestyle." We will go to whatever lengths to deflect blame and show that we are undeserving of God's wrath.

Verse 7 is an example of using any argument possible to do away with the fact that I am a sinner (and therefore doing away with guilt), to the effect, "Why am I still judged a sinner?" I suspect on a personal level we have each employed some form of this technique—anytime we've tried to rationalize going against our conscience. (e.g., "I'm not gossiping, I just feel you should know…" "This isn't anger, it's righteous indignation…" "What's wrong if it's not hurting anybody…," etc.). Some of us are so good at rationalizing, we're convinced we're not sinning.

The arguments Paul refers to, and all the justifications we've used, let's face it, are silly on their face. To all of us who have tried to rationalize away either God's justness to inflict wrath, or our sinfulness in deserving it, Paul concludes simply, *"Their condemnation is just."* Our self-defensive justifications provide divine evidence that our condemnation is deserved.

Behind both of Paul's examples is the bitterness toward God we still hear today. "I can't believe in a God who allows 'such pain in the world' . . . 'the innocent to suffer' . . . 'somebody to go to hell' . . . or, 'this to happen to me.'" As atheism is often just rationalization to live as one pleases, our rationalizations concerning sin and its penalties are equally insincere and weak.

Personal Reflection:

(Answer to yourself) What are some things that might be sin which you have rationalized recently? Were your arguments really good, or silly?

Further Thoughts:

Paul refers to arguments he had heard (3:5, 7) to the effect that "God is unjust to inflict wrath," and that He should have no right to "judge me a sinner." Arguments as if to say God is to blame.

In college we had to study Bertrand Russell's classic atheistic argument against God. It goes like this:

1. If God exists, he has to be all-powerful and all-good.

2. If He creates a world it has to be the best of all possible worlds, because if He's all-powerful He could and if he's all-good, He would.

3. This isn't the "best of all possible worlds," namely there is innocent suffering.

4. Therefore God does not exist.

Wow! I knew there was something wrong with the argument, but I hadn't had a course in logic. All I knew about formal logic was something like, if the premises were sound then the premised-based conclusion had to be correct. This was a tough one. I prayed. Somehow the Lord enabled me to discover C.S. Lewis at this time (what an answered prayer it turned out to be!). Lewis had debated Russell on this very argument and here's how he answered him.

Lewis said the first three premises were correct, but the conclusion did not necessarily follow. He added, "That God would have to create the 'best of all possible worlds' is correct. Further it is correct that this is *not* the 'best of all possible worlds.' Therefore this must be the best of all possible *ways* to get to the 'best of all possible worlds,' which is yet to come."

For me, that was genius. It speaks to the very heart of "theodicy," the problem of evil. It alludes to the idea of sovereignty including freewill (which we'll address later), and that a world with freewill is better than one without. It properly separates God from being the Cause of evil, by the implication that freewill creatures are its cause (Norman Geisler likes to say, "God creates the *fact* of freedom—a *good* thing; freewill creatures create the *acts* of freedom, which can be *good* or *bad*"). It also holds out hope that the best is yet to come, and this must be the *best way* to get there. After all, God would have to create the *best way* because if He's all-powerful He could and if He's all good, He would!

If you're rationalizing sin as if God made you do it, or in some other manner trying to show that the consequences of His wrath are unjust, you need to think again. If you are rationalizing your unbelief or spiritual hardness toward the

Lord because of bitterness toward Him, or because of a belief that blames God for innocent suffering, please reconsider your thinking! God gets wrongly blamed for too many things!

Group Questions:
1. Name two or three things considered sinful 40 years ago that are embraced as normal today.

2. Why is rationalization evidence of guilt? Why would Paul say to those rationalizing, "their condemnation is just?"

3. Why would we be rationalizing if we didn't feel guilty? (In case you skipped the last couple of readings, why do we feel "guilty?")

4. These thoughts on rationalizing/condemnation are fundamental for Paul. Later he will say, "Happy is he who does not *condemn* himself in what he approves. But he who doubts is *condemned already... whatever is not from faith is sin*" (Romans 14:22-23). Why is double-minded rationalization self-condemning in itself?

5. Have you known someone who is an atheist because they feel that if God exists there couldn't be so much innocent suffering? Have you known anyone to use that same argument to justify a sinful lifestyle?

5

Lying

"Let God be found true though every man a liar." Romans 3:4

Many of us have used or at least seen the gospel tract, *The Four Spiritual Laws*, or one of the many similar to it. These tracts usually have a section early on relating to the fact that each of us are sinners. In over thirty years of sharing the gospel I've met literally hundreds of people who took issue with one or more of the *"Four Spiritual Laws,"* but only two who disagreed with this point about being sinners. (The two of whom I refer were not only blowing smoke… In both cases, it was fairly obvious they smoked something else, and I don't mean cigarettes. No kidding, but that's another story).

Most folks readily admit they are sinners. They might debate the other points for some reason, but not many debate the general truth that they've sinned.

Sin is self-evident, as Paul shows in Romans 2–3. But times are changing. With shifts in worldviews happening more rapidly, "progressive thinking" is popular. Philosophies and psychologies are invented every day advocating that the very *idea* of "sin" is wrongheaded. "Why, what would such thinking do to a fragile self-image, if one thinks he's a *'sinner'?"*

Just ponder the title of a *chic* book recently seen in the hands of Hollywood trend setters, Demi Moore, Madonna, and Gwyneth Paltrow, *"Becoming Like God: Kabbalah And Our Ultimate Destiny."* Rather than thinking of ourselves as sinful, the trend is 180° the other way!

In a verse designed to set God apart as utterly true, trustworthy to keep His every promise, there is a negative but equal truth. "Let God be found true, *though every man a liar.*" We might be big sinners, little sinners, or live in the delusion that we have *no* sin, but the Bible says not only are we sinners but there is a specific sin that we've *all* committed—*lying!*

Do a survey on a group sometime. Tell them there is a sin that the Bible says each of us has committed. See if they can guess which one (I suppose there are others we've all done, but *for sure* we have all done this one in some fashion). I don't doubt some will guess it, but I'd like to hear the answers!

We might not think much about the sin of lying, *but God does.* In Proverbs, where so much is said about "dishonest scales," the value of integrity and honesty, Solomon mentions seven things the Lord hates. Only one is repeated. *Pride?* It's at the top, but no. *Shedding innocent blood?* Nope. *Sowing discord?* As terrible as it is, not that one either. The only one *repeated,* obviously so there is no mistake about what God really abhors, is *lying.* *"A lying tongue,"* God abhors, and *"a false witness who speaks lies"* (Prov 6:16-19). Lying is abominable to the Lord.

The Hollywood crowd thinking they are God, or *becoming* God, must not know the qualifications! *You can't lie!* They've lied! "Let God be found true, though every man a liar." If you run across someone who says he hasn't sinned, *he's lying!* (And ladies, though you might have concluded long ago that "every *man* (is) a liar," God does not let you off the generic hook!)

Personal Reflection:

Don't answer aloud, but ponder for a moment—are there any lies in your life right now?

Further Thoughts:

We can all think of our own examples of lying. When I was in high school my dad bought me a new car, a 1973 Capri. At a Friday night football game someone had knocked out the rear window and stolen my eight-track tape deck. I played on the golf team, so that Monday I was pulling out of the parking lot coming home after practice. Reaching behind my seat, while driving, I picked out pieces of glass still in the carpet. A shard cut my finger. Looking at the bleeding, I wasn't looking at the road. It curved one way and my car casually went the other. Up on the curve, through some trees (and over them) and onto number one fairway at Tenison Park! Talk about embarrassing.

I called for a wrecker, got it towed to a shop, and connived a way to get it fixed without my parents knowing. Fortunately my parents were out of town for a few days. A new radiator, wheel alignment, and a few other items amassed a bill of $332. I borrowed the money from an older friend, the work was done and I thought I was home free, just like Ferris Beuhler. I worked Saturdays to pay my friend back and actually thought my parents, if they had known, would be proud of me taking so much initiative and all.

Over a month passed and my friend was paid-off. All was right with the world. Until the afternoon my dad walked in the house. Having seen a small dent on the hood, the last remnant of my obstacle course exploits, he queried, "What happened?" I came clean, told him the whole thing, half-expecting him to be proud of me. Instead it was as somber as I'd ever seen my dad. He was *really* disappointed. More sad than mad. Not at all for my careless driving or for the wreck, but because I hadn't been honest and forthright about it. It hurt him, I think, that his son felt a need to be deceptive. "I just want you to be honest with me from now on," he said gently but ever so strongly. I got the message.

He didn't punish me or raise his voice. I felt I had let him down worse than anytime before. I might not have thought a lot about the cover-up, but he thought it was huge. To my knowledge, I never lied to him again. I didn't want to hurt him like that. I did other things that I thought were worse, like being smart-aleck or being disrespectful, but not being honest stands out as the time I hurt him worst of all.

We might not think lying is big, but God does. Wise people think it's big, too. Several years ago in *Fortune 500* a survey was done among the top fifty CEO's in the country. "What one quality is necessary to make it as a top CEO." Every answer dealt with honesty or integrity. "You might can make it in the 'small time,' being crooked or dishonest, but you'll never make it in the big time," was the consensus.

Howard Hendricks once reflected that of all the character qualities he could want for his kids, honesty was at the top— honesty with themselves, with others and with God.

Group Questions:

1. Without revealing too much, can you share a time with the group when you lied?

2. If God hates lying so much, what does it tell you about God?

3. Of all sins—and He hates them all—why is this one singled out as if for *extra* hatred? Why is lying so bad?

4. Have you been lied to by one of your children, a spouse, or a dear friend? How did it make you feel?

6

Powerless

*"Therefore by the works of the law
shall no flesh be justified in His sight,
for through the law comes the knowledge of sin."*
Romans 3:20

Maybe you've seen the funny scene in *Christmas With the Kranks* where Tim Allen has had Botox injections on his face. Puffed-up like a balloon ready to break, the comedian's normally animated facial features are expressionless due to the temporary deadening of Botox paralysis. Bites of food keep falling out. Funny in the film, but in real life paralysis is no laughing matter.

Sin is like a paralyzing "drug." We are deceived into thinking it will make life more fun and beautiful, but the paralysis it inflicts is not temporary.

We are all spiritual paralytics because of sin. We are impotent, "helpless," "without strength," "powerless," Paul will say later (5:6). Too helpless and weak to make ourselves right with God. Even trying to be as good as we can won't do it, for *"by the works of the law shall no flesh be justified in His sight."* Though we might not keep the law *perfectly*, we'd like to think God grades on the curve. He doesn't. We hope it's like balancing scales—if our good works outweigh our bad, then He'll say we're okay. It doesn't work that way either.

One super-hip high schooler expressed to me a while back what I think is the *ethos* of the age. He felt God was a Universal Spirit. There is no hell. This Universal Spirit wouldn't send anyone to hell, and if He did, it would only be for *really bad* sinners, "like murderers." He didn't think it would be right for God to send him to hell for the "little" sins *he* did.

"What's your *basis* for believing in this God?," I asked. He had none; it's just what he *felt*. Many have similar feelings, though lacking an objective basis for them. The fact is, this fellow is a regular user, sexually active, a popular guy and great athlete. He's an example of one's morality dictating his theology. Too often we, too, create a God in our own image who allows us to do what we want. For my young friend, it matters little that his "God" is *only in his imagination*—it is the "God" he *wants* to exist. We might want God to grade on the curve, but that's not the objective God of reality.

The God of the Bible—who provides so much objective data about Himself—says we are not doers of the law, but *breakers of it*. Further, Jesus' own brother, James, says, "Whoever keeps the whole law, and yet *stumbles at one point*, he has become *guilty of all*," hastening to add, and "*we all* stumble in *many* (points)" (Jas 2:10; 3:2). *Guilty of all* implies deserving of the consequences of all as well, some of which required the death penalty. Paul has already said as much in 1:32, after a lengthy list of various sins, "who, knowing the righteous requirement of God, that those who practice such things are *worthy of death*, not only do the same but also approve of those who practice them." The God of the Bible, unlike so many

40

"gods" of this age, says we have broken the law and deserve death.

The law was never intended to constitute us righteous, but to *condemn us,* "for through the law comes the knowledge of sin." Paul will say this again to the Galatians, "That no one is justified by the law is evident. . . If there had been a law given which *could have given life,* truly righteousness (viz., justification) would have been by the law" (Gal 3:21). Instead, by showing us that we are sinners, and that the law can't remedy our predicament, it shows us our need for a Savior, "the law is a tutor to bring us to Christ" (Gal 3:24).

In and of itself, the law is also powerless to save us. "For what the law could not do, *weak as it was* through the flesh, *God did…*" Concerning justification, we're powerless. The law is powerless. But God and His Gospel are strong. What *God did* and has provided, is *much more* than what you might think. He has the cure for our weakness, "helplessness," our spiritual, sin-injected paralysis. Stay tuned.

Personal Reflection:

Powerless, helpless, weak... why God would describe us in such terms?

Further Thoughts:

There is a commonly recurring dream among the human species. Generally set in a fearful, or potentially fearful situation, but particular to the individual. For a ballplayer it might be dreaming that regardless of the effort, and even with his best hit, the ball just doesn't go anywhere.

Many have testified to the dream of being chased by something sinister, yet totally unable to run away, or unable to run swift enough… as though the shoes had lead weights.

Women often speak of a dream (I've had it, too) where something terrible or life-threatening is occurring and try as they might to scream, nothing comes out! (Usually followed by waking one's self, as well as the spouse, with a loud shout!— Have you ever had that happen?)

I used to dream about a drunk burglar I couldn't beat-up. Deadened by drink, my best hits didn't phase him.

Powerlessness. Impotency. Weakness. Paralysis. Inability. Things of which nightmares are made. The fact is, spiritually, that's where we are. The law is weak. You're weak. I'm weak. Powerless to make ourselves right with God. "They are weak but He is strong," rightly goes the song. Christ is infinitely strong. In short order, Paul will tell us what Christ did for us for us that, in our weakness, we couldn't for ourselves.

Group Questions:

1. Have you ever had temporary paralysis—maybe even the numbness from the dentist. What was it like?

2. How is sin like a paralyzing drug?

3. Romans 5:6 is translated in various ways, "For when we were still *without strength*" (NKJV); "While we were *helpless*" (NASB); "when we were still *powerless*" (NIV). The word *astheneō* means to be *weak, sick, powerless*; it refers to a bodily ailment or disease, but could be used of one who is "*weak in faith*" or "*in need*" economically. Read 5:6 and describe what our "weakness" is in relation to. What are the ramifications of our "powerlessness"?

4. The same word used in Romans 5:6 to describe our weakness is used in Romans 8:3 to say, "What the law could not do, *weak (astheneō)* as it was through the flesh, God did, sending His own Son…"). How is the law "*weak*"?

5. The law is not able to justify us, but it can do *some things*. What are some of those things; what is the purpose of the law?

7

Death

"For all have sinned and fall short of the glory of God." Romans 3:23

A little fellow went to church by himself one Sunday. When he came home the parents asked what the preacher had preached on. "Sin," came the short reply, not losing a step, but shedding no further light. "Well what did he say about sin, honey?" "He's against it." Unfortunately, too many sermons could be summed-up that simply, as if they're all about that one three-letter word. Beginning in the next reading we'll go on to some of the greatest, most loveable, life-changing topics of the Bible, but one last thing about that three-lettered word.

The summation of this first section, "Bad News," is in this verse, *"for all have sinned and fall short of the glory of God."* Understood in it, of course, is what he well says later, interestingly in the Christian-life section of Romans, *"the wages of sin is death"* (6:23). Paul has been clear, hammering home in various ways that we all, Jew or Gentile, with or without the law, *all of us* have *sinned* and that those who do such things, are *"deserving of death"* (1:32). Whether with or without exposure to God's revelation, we have all broken God's universal internal law written in our hearts, and will *perish* for it (2:12).

The word *perish* conjures up our worst fears about death. Just the sound of it. It means to be ruined, destroyed, to die. *Perish* almost sounds similar to disa*ppear*. I don't know if the words are related, but listen to what James says about actually *perishing*—"For what is your life? It is even a vapor that *appears* for a little time and then *vanishes away*" (Jas 4:14). Perishing... dying... disappearing. You are here for a little while, then "poof," you are going to *"vanish away."* Vanish to where? Vanish into what? I don't like it... I don't like the sound of it. I don't think you do either.

What is *Death?* Fundamentally, it is *separation*, "the body without the spirit is *dead"* (Jas 2:26). Someone has well said, *"Physical death* is separation of the spirit from the body. *Spiritual death* is separation of the person from God (Jn 5:24). *Eternal death*, the *'second death,'* takes place after the Great White Throne Judgment." People whose names are not written in the Book of Life will be judged according to their deeds and "cast into the lake of fire," eternally separated from God (Rev 20:11-15).

Physical death, spiritual death, eternal death... Quit trying to scare me, you say. I'm not trying to, these are just realities. Obviously, *physical* death exists. All that's left to debate is why. *Spiritual* death is fairly undeniable when we think of its universal effects—varying shades of guilt, depression, shame, isolation, despair, condemnation, misery, etc. Don't call it *"spiritual death"* if you like, but the phenomenon is there nevertheless. All that remains is *eternal death*, which has to be taken on faith, and depends on what you think about the reliability of the Bible as "God's Word" which discusses it.

Hopefully you are as ready as I am to see what this "gospel" in Romans is about—how we can be saved, through God's power, by believing. Saved from death? from wrath? from judgment? How? Here we go...

Personal Reflection:

What aspect of death do you hate the most? The Scriptures say God hates death, too. Why would He hate it?

Further Thoughts::

Being the youngest in my family, and of parents who were the youngest and second to youngest in theirs, I've unfortunately had to see too many dearly loved grandparents, aunts, uncles cousins, my mom and dad, and even a brother... die. I hate it. Cried every time.

Having gone to seminary I'm dubbed the family "minister" for these funerals. On one hand, I'm so thankful for an opportunity to remind family and friends of our wonderful Gospel—the assuring faith and hope it gives. I never weary of reminding them of that. But on the other hand, I hate that such events ever had to be in the first place. I *hate* death. I'm sure you do, too. God hates it too! "I have no pleasure in the death of one who dies" (Ezek 18:32). Unlike many of us, God takes no pleasure even when the *wicked* die (Ezek 18:23)! We might be glad, say, were Osama bin Laden killed, or some other terrorist or really *wicked* person. God actually hates death more than we do!

We will see shortly that God's present wrath includes another classification of death—the death-type experience of a believer who possesses eternal life but *experiences* "death" *here and now*—part of the present condemning consequences of sin. God does not want that for His children. The full and final answer for our deliverance awaits us in the next three sections.

Group Questions:

1. For most people death has an element of scariness and fear. Why?

2. What were the three types of death we mentioned? And the fourth?

3. Why do you hate death?

4. Whether one has the law or not, he is going to "perish" (2:12)? What does this mean and why is it so?

Section II

Romans 3:21–4:25

Good News: Justification

*"Therefore having been justified by faith
we have peace with God
through our Lord Jesus Christ."*

Romans 5:1

8

Justification
(Suggested Reading, Romans 3-4)

> *"Being justified freely by His grace*
> *through the redemption that is in Christ Jesus…"*
> Romans 3:24

Most of you reading this can probably quote Romans 3:23, one of the first destinations on the *Roman Road of Salvation,* "For all have sinned and fallen short of the glory of God…"   Can you complete the remainder of the verse? All the best translations have 3:23 ending with a comma and continuing into 3:24 and beyond. This is the beginning of the dynamite power of God unto salvation Paul mentioned at the beginning. The verse continues, "(B)eing justified freely by His grace through the redemption that is in Christ Jesus." It is a loaded summary for this section through 5:9-10, and an important building block crucial to understanding the entire book.

"Justification" (*dikaioō*) was a legal term meaning to *declare or pronounce as righteous; to vindicate, treat as just.* Imagine a courtroom setting and the person on trial is acquitted. The charges will not be held against him. He is *declared righteous* by the judge. (It may seem of little importance presently, but it is important to know, and will come up later, that the word strictly means to be *declared* righteous, not *made* righteous. Though a person is *declared* and treated as justified from the moment of faith, the believer may not *live* "righteously" for years. No believer will live a perfectly righteous life until he gets to heaven. Until then he is nevertheless in "right standing" with God through justification.)

As Judge, God has the hardest job in the world. How can He remain "just and yet the justifier?" (Ro 3:26). If He's "just," He can't lower His righteous standard. He can't just wink His eye with the attitude, "Boys will be boys," or, "Let's let bygones be bygones," and forgive us willy nilly. Why? Because God is just and He can't change. Along with that, He can't lie (remember, "Let God be found true though every man a liar," of 3:4? "God cannot lie," Titus 1:2, etc.). He promised the death penalty for sin. He can't lie. He can't change. (His righteous standards come from His righteous, unchanging nature.) So death it must be.

Then how can He justify us if He's going to remain just? You've heard the old illustration of the guilty party who has a fine to pay, and no money to pay it. The good judge can't just waive it—but he *can* pay it himself. And in our case the payment was most supreme—the death of His "only begotten," our Lord and Savior Jesus Christ. He died our death. He took our punishment. He paid the sin debt against us in full. That's how God can remain "just and yet the justifier of the one who has faith in Jesus" (3:26).

Further, that's how we are "justified *freely* by His *grace*." It's "*through the redemption* that is in Christ Jesus." *Freely.* It costs us nothing, though it cost Him unfathomably. If anyone ever hints to you that eternal right standing before God costs *you* a-n-y-t-h-i-n-g, *anything* at all, you better run!

51

Personal Reflection:

1. In light of this, why did Christ die for us?

2. If Christ has truly paid the redemption price for our justification, why do so many act or speak as if there is still a cost on our part? What are some ways preachers or evangelists might tack on a cost to this free justification?

Further Thoughts:

The story goes in the days of old, of a Russian Czar named Nicholas II. There was a food shortage and someone was pilfering the bread. Unable to discover the culprit, the Czar decreed thirty lashes for anyone caught pilfering the bread.

A few days later and the authorities nabbed the evil doer, bread in hand. It was the Czar's own elderly mother!

Of course the Czar did not want his mother to receive the lashes. Yet, to be fair and just, he must. It wouldn't be right to "forgive," knowing he likely wouldn't forgive others. Indeed under the circumstances this case was more serious than just stealing bread. No, the Czar's word had to stand for something.

Perplexed about the possibility of his beloved mother taking the lashes, he knew there was only one thing to do. Take her place. In this way, His word would be true, and he could remain just and fair.

The day came and he took her lashes. He was already well-loved. This made him more so.

Reflective of what the Lord has done for us, but paling in comparison, God offered not His own life for us but something more, the life of His dear Son. His Word does mean something. He remains just and yet the Justifier. "We are justified *freely* by His grace through the redemption that is in Christ Jesus."

Group Questions:

1. One need not go back to Nicholas II for an illustration of being justified freely. Can you name a time when someone took the fall for you so you could get off the hook?

2. If Christ has truly paid the redemption price for our justification, why do so many act or speak as if there is still a cost on our part to be declared righteous? What are some ways in which you have heard preachers or evangelists subtly tack on a cost to this free justification?

3. Why is the distinction important between being "declared righteous" and "made righteous?" That "*justified*" is past tense, what does that imply?

9

Grace

*"Being justified freely by His grace
through the redemption that is in Christ Jesus."*
Romans 3:24

Justification is free to us because it is "by His *grace* through the redemption that is in Christ Jesus." The word *charis* means *grace, favor, graciousness* and is as multi-hued as our word *grace* itself. It is able to signify the beauty of an act, or the gracious character behind it. It can describe the beautiful, flowingly smooth movement of an athlete, "*She did that with such grace*," or it can mean benevolence, help, or enablement. Grace has beautiful and broad meanings, but throughout *Romans* its meaning is very specific.

Usage and context always determines the meaning of a word. Paul chooses the beautiful word *charis* but infuses it with a technical meaning throughout the book. In *Romans* it simply means *gift* or *favor*, as opposed to something earned or deserved. We know this because of how Paul defines and uses it throughout the book. For example, emphasizing that justification is by grace through faith, and that it most certainly is not of works, he says,

> *"Now to him who works, the wages are not counted as grace [gift, favor] but as debt [what is due, merited, earned]"* (4:4)

"Therefore it [justification] is of faith (not works) that it might be according to grace..." (4:16)

"And if by grace, then it is no longer of works; otherwise grace is no longer grace. But if it is of works, it is no longer of grace; otherwise work is no longer work" (11:6)

The fundamental thought in Paul's mind about grace in the book of Romans is that *"grace" and "works" are mutually exclusive.* So as to make it unmistakable, he puts Romans 11:6 (above) in the form of a logical syllogism that cannot be misinterpreted.

Years ago we had a kid in Young Life who fell in love with the Gospel of grace. It set him free! For the first time, he knew he was going to heaven, that he was justified before God, not by anything he had done but totally through what Christ had done in his place. So excited, he shared this with his brother. "Wait a minute," the brother skeptically replied, "there are a million different interpretations on any given verse... who's to know the right one? Only the priest can tells us."

Some verses *are* difficult, but "the main things are the plain things and the plain things are the main things." This is a MAIN thing! And so we do not miss it, God puts in a Romans 11:6—and many more just like it through the New Testament—verses that cannot be misinterpreted. Grace is mutually exclusive with works. If I have to raise even my little finger, then "it is of works, and no longer of grace." ...No wonder this justification before God is given *freely*! It's *by grace*, apart from works!

Personal Reflection:

Why do you suppose so many of the world, even in "Christendom," want to work so hard to be justified before God when it is free?

Further Thoughts:

In *The Great Divorce*, a bus ride from hell to heaven, C.S. Lewis describes one of the men eager for the next bus back. Shortly after arrival in heaven one of the visitors—the Big Man, Lewis calls him—sees someone he knew on earth, "Well I'll be damned." Turned out to be a fellow who worked under him named Len. "It isn't right, you know... What about poor Jack?" Turns out Len had murdered Jack back on earth. "Jack is here. You'll meet him soon if you stay," replied Len. "But you murdered him," Big Man said. "Of course I did... but it's all right now."

"All right for *you*... But what about the poor chap himself, laying cold and dead?," Big Man grumps. "But he isn't... you'll meet him soon...," his heavenly host rejoins, and shares a little of what happened to him after the murder. How he had "given-up" on himself and how that was when everything began...

The Big Man would have none of it, filled with self-pride he goes off on Len. "Look at me," he said slapping his chest, "I gone straight all my life. I don't say I was a religious man and I don't say I had no faults, far from it. But I done my best all my life, see? I done my best by everyone, that's the sort of chap I was. I never asked for anything... If I wanted a drink

I paid for it and if I took my wages I done my job, see? That's the sort I was and I don't care who knows it."

Len encourages him not to go on like that. "Who's going on? I'm asking for nothing but my rights..." Len tries to explain that we shouldn't want our *rights*, "You'll get something far better." Like the Pharisee and tax-collector, Big Man insists, "I haven't got my rights. I always done my best and I never done nothing wrong... I don't see why I should be put below a bloody murderer like you." Len tries to lead him, "Who knows whether you will be? Only be happy and come with me."

"...I only want my rights. I'm not asking for anybody's bleeding charity." "Then do, at once, Ask for the Bleeding Charity. Everything is here for the asking and nothing can be bought," says Len. Big Man persists, "If they choose to let in a bloody murderer all because he cries poor mouth at the last moment... I don't see myself going in the same boat with you. Why should I? I don't want charity. I'm a decent man and if I had my rights I'd have been here long ago."

With mirth in his eyes, Len corrects him, "It isn't exactly true... You weren't a decent man and you didn't do your best. We none of us were and we none of us did..." Len explained how murdering Jack wasn't the worse thing he did. He was half mad when he did that act in the heat of the moment. Fact is, the hatred and anger he regularly harbored, even toward the Big Man, was worse.

"It's all a clique, a bloody clique," the Big Man concludes. "Tell them I'm not coming, see? I'd rather be damned than go along with you. I came to get my rights... not to go along on charity. I'll go home. That's what I'll do. Damn and blast the whole pack of you."

———

I know a lady who is a champion for grace. Talking about her to a mutual friend, the friend confided to me, "I'll tell you why Shirley is so big on grace. Years ago she left her husband for another man. The boyfriend eventually dropped her. She went back to her husband. *He took her back.* That's why she's so big on 'grace.'" I didn't quite know how to read my friend's comments. Certainly it's a horrible thing that Shirley left her husband. But that doesn't impugn *grace*. The fact is, we've all done as badly as Shirley, though maybe in different ways. We all need grace! Paul was such a champion of grace partly because he felt his own sinfulness so keenly, "I'm the chief of sinners," he said.

Group Questions:

1. Name a few things you have received that were absolutely free.

2. Can you name something someone has given you, which was unmerited, you didn't work for, had no strings attached, and came from pure grace on the part of the giver?

3. Why do you think so many, even in "Christendom," resist the concept of free grace in the Gospel?

4. The western culture has rightly esteemed the value of hard work. "If it's worth having, it's worth working for," or,

"Nothing in life is free." Can you give examples of when those quotes are actually false?

5. Why is Romans 11:6 impossible to misinterpret? In Romans, what is Paul's most "fundamental thought" concerning "grace"?

10

Redemption

"Being justified freely by His grace
through the redemption that is in Christ Jesus."
Romans 3:24

There are several verbs translated *"redeem"* in the New Testament: *agōrazō*—to buy at the "agora," or marketplace; *exagōrazō*—to buy-out-from the market place; and *lutroō*—to loose by a price. Concerning the first two, what often went on at the agora or forum, as you might remember from the movie *Gladiator*, was the buying and selling of slaves.

Sometimes slaves were bought and turned loose, especially if they happened to be your relative, as in the story of Hosea and his wife Gomer. *Lutroō* especially fits here. The first two words emphasize the "buying" aspect of redemption, like "You have been *bought with a price (agōrazō),* therefore glorify God with your body…" (I Cor 6:20). The latter emphasizes the freeing/loosing aspect, as in I Peter 1:18-19, "knowing that you were not *redeemed (lutroō)* with perishable things like silver and gold from your futile way of life…but with the precious blood, as of a lamb unblemished and spotless, the blood of Christ." But all these verbs include both the buying and loosing aspect of *redemption*.

The noun *redemption* comes from one of two similar words related to *lutroō*, the nouns *lutrōsis* and *apolutrōsis* (understood to mean *redemption*, literally they are *loosing* and *loosing away*). A third word in the family is *lutron*, ransom, "For even the Son of Man did not come to be served, but to serve, and to give His life a *ransom (lutron)* for many" (Mk 10:45).

Gomer, the wife of Hosea the prophet, was unfaithful... just like Israel was to the Lord. Hosea's everlasting, gracious love for her depicted that of the Lord for His people. Hosea, like the Lord with wayward Israel, did not force Gomer to love him. Persistent, with brokenhearted love, he tried to woo and win her back...

From a distance he watched as she went from one lover to the next, breaking his heart. He loved her so much, unbeknownst to her he provided for her needs. She assumed the provisions were from her lovers. . . as Israel thought her blessings came from the various idols she served. Gomer "behaved shamefully". . . "I will go after my lovers, who gave me my bread and my water, my wool and my linen, my oil and my drink." If that weren't bad enough, listen to some of the saddest words in all the Scriptures. . . *"But Me she forgot,"* says the Lord (2:13)...

Things got so bad for Gomer—when you sow to the wind, you reap a whirlwind—she ended-up on the scaffel being sold as a slave. Hosea paid the redemption price, fifteen shekels of silver and change. God would one day pay the redemption price for His people Israel... and you and me. A price far more precious than "silver and gold," Peter reminds, *"the precious blood of an unblemished and spotless Lamb."*

Grace is not cheap. For justification to be absolutely free to us, the redemption cost to Christ had to be very great.

Personal Reflection:

1. Some credit their boss, their spouse, their own hard work. Whom do you give credit for the various blessings in your life?

2. *"But Me she forgot"*—can that ever be said about you? How often and in what ways do you forget God?

3. What do you think about God's redeeming you?

Further Thoughts:
When I was a kid "S&H Green Stamps" were big. Some stores gave them out depending on how much you'd buy. There were "Green Stamp" catalogs with all kinds of neat items for adults or kids, and "redemption" stores where you could trade-in your stamps for the items you picked.

My friends and I were quite the hunters in the fields behind our houses—at least in our seven year-old imaginations. I envisioned the bow and arrow set in the catalog as my ticket to hunting stardom.

The day came when I finally filled six and one-half books of Green Stamps, just the amount for the bow set. Redeeming the bow with those books was one of the fond days of my early life. Almost as fun as when, shortly after, I shot that rabbit from near point-blank range, right in front of my friends. Bullseye!

Two things happened in the blink of an eye. First, I imagined my friends hoisting me to their shoulders as the warrior-hero of our block. Second, I watched as the arrow bounced harmlessly off the rabbit. Totally un-phased he hopped off to laugh with his family I presume, just as my friends were heartily laughing with me. I perceived quickly, if I had killed the rabbit, it would've killed *me!* I'm not a hunter.

God is *pleased* to have allowed His Son to pay the redemption price (Is 53:10). He is *thrilled* when we accept by faith that He has made that payment for us. His payment was way more than six and one-half books of stamps; His purchase a lot more valuable than a bow and arrow set. (We are worth an immeasurable amount to our Lord!) As we'll see later, He will wield us far more effectively than I did my bow set. But unlike the bow set, we'll have a role to play in that; we'll have a say in whether we allow Him to use us or not.

Group Questions:

1. Have you ever "redeemed" something? What?

2. Thinking back to Hosea, have you had a loved-one, perhaps a spouse, parent or child, who broke your heart? In what ways have *you* broken God's heart? Do you think God has made efforts to woo and win you back? In what ways?

3. What does God's redemption provide for us?

4. Knowing what He has done for us, what should be our response?

11

Propitiation

"whom God set forth as a propitiation by His blood, through faith…"
Romans 3:25

"*And He Himself (Christ) is the propitiation for our sins, and not for ours only but also for the whole world*" (I Jn 2:2). The word "propitiation" in the ancient world meant the "appeasing or satisfying of a wrathful deity." The NIV translates it *atoning sacrifice*. While some are uncomfortable with a God who can get angry, nevertheless the Bible portrays God as "wrathful" concerning our sins (cf. Rom 1:18; 2:5). Christ's substitutionary death has fully appeased, satisfied, that wrath on our behalf.

Dr. Ryrie used to say when teaching on propitiation, "So when you are sharing the Gospel, don't give anyone a chance to get in on *propitiating* God… *Christ has already fully propitiated Him.*" What he meant was, do not communicate to the person that raising a hand, walking an aisle, repenting, or even saying a prayer is something that needs to be added to Christ's finished work on the cross. Christ's death has fully satisfied God and made payment for our sins. All we do, as the New Testament says over 150 times, is receive what He has done for us by faith (Jn 3:16; Eph 2:8-9, etc.)

This idea so moved one of our Young Life leaders years ago that he made a talk on it and gave one of the greatest illustrations I've ever heard. When Tommy was in high school he dated a beautiful girl named Edie. It was homecoming day and he had brought the mum over to her house that morning, looking forward to the dance that night. Tommy was really proud of the mum. He had not only paid a good price, he personally designed it himself—every detail. It wasn't the ordinary mum, it was his artistic masterpiece.

That night when he went to pick-up Edie, she met him at the door, beautiful as ever, but his mum had grown twice as large! Maybe she wasn't quite satisfied. She had taken it to Flowers By Cheryl and had some things added to it! "I didn't know whether to spit or cry," Tommy says years later still feeling the emotion. "I was sad and angry at the same time." He added, *"It was like a slap in my face."*

Pausing, he made his point, "But that's exactly what we do to the Lord when we act like there's something we need to add to Christ's finished work on our behalf. Christ's death has fully and forever satisfied God's wrath against us. Nothing needs to be added. We need to understand that *He* is our propitiation. We simply receive what He has done with the empty hands of faith."

Personal Reflection:

Do you believe that Christ death has fully satisfied God's wrath for your sins? What difference should that make in your life?

Group Questions:

1. Have you ever had something in your life that made you
    sad and angry at the same time?

2. Why would Tommy say that adding conditions on the
    reception of the gospel is a "slap in God's face?"

3. Why is simple faith the appropriate response; why not
    repentance, confession, or some other good works?

12

Righteousness

(Suggested Reading, Romans 4)

"But to him who does not work but believes on Him who justifies the ungodly, his faith is accounted for righteousness, just as David also describes the blessedness of the man to whom God imputes righteousness apart from works." Roman 4:5-6

This section on justification actually begins in 3:21, "But now the *righteousness of God* apart from the law is revealed... even the *righteousness of God* through faith in Jesus Christ, to all and on all who believe" (3:21-22). This marks the beginning of the revelation he promised in the summary heading of the book, "For in [this gospel] the *righteousness of God* is revealed from faith to faith: as it is written, 'The just shall live by faith'" (1:17). And he will come back to it later, when Paul says Israel's zeal for God is undirected by knowledge, "For they are ignorant of *God's righteousness*, and seeking to establish their own righteousness, have not submitted to the *righteousness of God*. For Christ is the end of the law for righteousness to everyone who believes" (10:3-4).

Righteousness and *justification* are sister and brother, *dikaiosunē* and *dikaioō*. The former means *uprightness, justice, righteousness*. The latter, as we have mentioned, is a forensic term meaning *to be declared righteous*. When we believe in Jesus Christ we get both. We are *declared righteous* and we are given "righteousness." In fact Christ's very own righteousness is *imputed*, or *reckoned,* to our account. As Paul said, "The righteousness of God is revealed... to all and *on all* who believe" (3:21-22).

The person who *"does not work"* but simply *"believes"* on Him who justifies the ungodly, his faith is *accounted* (*logizetai*) for righteousness." He goes on to describe the joy and peace "of the man to whom God *imputes* (*logizetai*) righteousness apart from works."

Both "accounted" and "imputes" translates the same exact word and tense, from *logizomai*—to reckon or calculate. It's a simple arithmetic word. God looks at the accounts. We have a debt we could never pay. Christ paid it, so it "adds-up" that we are righteous; He "reckons" us righteous—literally, he *calculates* it—when we believe Him for what Christ has done for us.

This righteousness that God gives the believer by faith is emphatically *"apart from works!"* In fact, it can be implied that a person who is trusting in Christ *and*   (fill-in the blank)   to be made right with God has missed the boat. If the *"and __"* is not simply a synonym for believing in Christ, almost certainly it will be some kind of *"work"*—repenting, persevering, being "committed," "obeying" Him, etc.[2] As Paul will say, if those things are added, why did Christ need to die? *Just do those things!* "I do not nullify the *grace* of God, for if *righteousness* comes through the law, then Christ died needlessly" (Gal 2:21). He wrote that to correct this very problem. False teachers had crept in saying one needs to "believe in Christ *and* ____" to be righteous. When Paul says,

"We maintain that man is justified by faith apart from works of the law" (3:28; Gal 2:16, Phil 3:9, et al), he has first in mind *apart* from works of the Jewish law, but also *apart* from any manmade law, and as seen here in 4:5-6, apart from *any works* period!

Personal Reflection:

1. Have you trusted in a "Christ and ____" gospel? If so, Christ and what?

2. Do you now trust in a "Christ alone" gospel? What influenced you to do so?

Further Thoughts:

I'll never forget Guy Owen being so descript, explaining that "all our righteousness are like filthy rags" (Is 64:6). When he was finished with us, there was no uncertainty whether "our" filthy-rags righteousness was good enough to satisfy God.

I'll also never forget Mark Hines' illustration, as he took a crooked, wrinkled piece of string, so jagged compared to the straight-edged ruler to which he held it. The ruler represented God's righteous standard, the crooked string our righteousness. Then he took his hard-backed Bible, representing Christ, and placed the string *in the Bible.* He held the Bible next to the straight-edge and it *did match-up.* It was as straight as the ruler. "God has placed us *in* Christ," he explained, "and given His righteousness to us. 'He made Him who knew no sin *to be sin*, in order that we might be the righteousness of God *in Him*' (2 Co 5:21). He took our sin and gave us His righteousness."

Maybe you are in business and appreciate "ledger sheet" language, "credits on the left, debits on the right" (*I think that's correct*—I passed accounting only because they graded on the curve!) God looks at the ledger sheet, our sins, our "filthy rags righteousness," on the debit side; *nothing* from our account on the credit side. God looks at the death of His Son, and stamps *"Tetelestai,"* on the balance sheet (or invoice), *"Paid-In-Full."* Then He takes His Divine accounting pen and writes in *"Christ's righteousness"* to our credit account.

(The teacher asked the first-grade class, "Is there anything God cannot do?" A wise little fellow said, "He can't see my sins through the blood of Jesus Christ.")

Group Questions:

1. Have you ever had something put into your account that you didn't earn? ...Have you ever been regarded more highly than you deserved?

2. Why do you think a person's *faith* is "reckoned" or "accounted" as righteousness? Why would God choose *faith* as the qualification to be accounted as righteous?

3. Have you ever had trouble reconciling your bank statement? Apart from Christ, should people have similar anxieties and frustrations with their lives not matching-up? Why or why not? How might you explain God's "accounting" practices to someone?

13

Faith

"But now the righteousness of God apart from the law is revealed…
through faith in Jesus Christ, to all and on all who believe."
Romans 3:21-22

At every turn in Romans is the concept of "faith." "For in it," Paul says of this gospel, "the righteousness of God is revealed from *faith* to *faith*; as it is written, 'The just shall live by *faith*'" (Ro 1:17). Notice, he does not stop mentioning faith!: "A propitiation… through *faith*… to demonstrate His righteousness, that He might be just and the justifier of the one who has *faith* in Jesus… Where is the boasting? It is excluded…by a 'law' of *faith*. Therefore we conclude that a man is justified by *faith* apart from works of the law… There is one God who will justify by *faith*…and through *faith*… Abraham *believed* God and it was accounted to him for righteousness… But to him who does not work but *believes* on Him who justifies the ungodly, his *faith* is accounted for righteousness…" etc.

The noun faith (*pistis*) and the verb believe (*pisteuô*) are used 37 and 20 times respectively thru Romans—57 times. The noun means *faith*, belief; the verb means *to believe*. The meanings are fairly narrow. Don't let anyone tell you that the Biblical word for faith means something other than faith!

These Greek words are a one-to-one equivalent to our words faith and believe.

Why does God choose to save us by *faith*? One thing is sure, faith is not a work: "It is by *faith* that it might be *in accordance with grace*" (4:16). God has chosen to save us by grace to exclude our pride and boasting (see 3:27; 4:2; Eph 2:8-9). He has chosen "the message of the cross"—foolishness to some, a stumbling block to others—to save those who *believe* it, "that no flesh should glory in His presence... but just as it is written, 'Let him who boasts, boast only in the Lord'" (I Cor 1:18-31). This "salvation-by-grace-through-faith" is not of works "lest any man should boast" (Eph 2:8-9).

If faith is *according to grace* and *not of works*, what exactly is it? It is the persuasion that something or someone is true or trustworthy. Fundamentally, it is passive. That is, by my volition I cannot will myself to believe what I don't believe. "Trust," a similar word on the other hand, might imply volition, but faith is something prior to that kind of "trust" (used in this manner, you *trust* something because you *believe* in it, that is, you believe certain things about it, so it is worthy of your "trust"). When Christ says to Martha, "Do you believe Me that all you have to do is believe Me and I will give you eternal life?" she either believes or she doesn't. If she does, there is no work at all on her part and, further, she has eternal life!

Faith is knowledge and certainty but *without sight*, "faith is the substance of things hoped for, the evidence of things *not seen*" (Heb 11:1). "We walk by faith, *not by sight*," (2 Cor 5:7). Faith and doubt are diametrically opposed. If one doubts, he is not believing and *vice versa* (see Mt 14:31; Mk 11:23; Rom 14:23; Jas 1:6). So, again, when Jesus says, "Whoever believes in Me has eternal life," if you believe Him, then you know you have eternal life; if you don't know you have eternal life, you are not believing Him.

Personal Reflection:

1. Why does the Bible say, do you think, "without faith it is impossible to please God?"

2. "The just shall live by faith," what does that mean to you?

Further Thoughts:

If I asked you, "Do you believe in China?" You'd probably answer yes. Even if you haven't been there, you might have many good reasons to believe it exists. Mainly, you probably just take it on good authority. The same faith with which you believe China exists, is no different than the kind of faith the Bible speaks of for justification or receiving eternal life. Faith is faith! Jesus says, "Most assuredly I say to you, whoever believes in Me has eternal life." You either believe it or you don't. There is no different kind of faith necessary for salvation than the faith we use in every day life.

Do not be suckered into the teaching that there is a difference between "heart faith" and "head faith." There is no difference; faith is faith. Faith always ultimately deals with propositions—statements. If you "believe Jim," "or believe *in* Jim," it is simply short for the proposition, "I believe *that*

(Jim) is telling me the truth," or "I believe *that* Jim is truthful," or "I believe *that* Jim is reliable."

Some argue that faith is not "intellectual assent to the facts," *but that is precisely what faith is!* Because of a misunderstanding of James 2:14-26 they suppose saving faith must have an element of commitment, or must be evidenced by works.[2] So, they'll often make a big deal that there is a difference between "believing *in*" and "believing *that*," the former implying some kind of subjective commitment more than simple faith; the latter implying simply assenting to facts being true. Yet, when Jesus tells Martha the Gospel in John 11:25, that He guarantees resurrection and eternal life to whomever believes Him for it, He asks, "Do you believe *this* (i.e., this set of facts)?" Uncorrected, she replies, "Yes I believe *that*."

In fact, John's purpose statement—the only book of the Bible written to non-Christians to tell them how to get eternal life—says "saving faith" is *precisely* mental assent to a certain set of *facts* as being true! "But these are written that you might *believe that* Jesus is the Christ... and *that* believing you may have life in His name" (Jn 20:31). "Believing *in*" Jesus is the same thing as "believing *that* Jesus is the Christ..." It's simply a shorthand version of John's fuller statement. In fact, John uses several variations of *believe* interchangeably, *believe in*, *whoever believes* (or the *one who believes*), *believing*, *believe that*, or simply *believe(s)*...

———

Some who don't think faith is that simple have come up with clever illustrations, like the "chair," the "elevator," or the "tight-roper," each loaded with theological gobbelty-goop.

Each implies that simple faith—assent to something being true or trustworthy—is not enough. They imply there's a mysterious subjective element in addition to belief that needs to be added. (I say *"mysterious,"* because rarely do they come out and say *exactly what it is* more than faith they want... But it's *something* more, some kind of commitment *beyond simple faith*, though usually stopping short of saying outright "works" and "obedience" as that would immediately smell of rottenness).

The "chair" illustration says, "Here's a chair. Do you believe this chair will hold you up? (Yes) Then you must get *'in'* the chair, because faith alone (or 'intellectual assent') is not enough." The "elevator" illustration says, "Here's an elevator that will take you to heaven. Do you believe it? (Yes) Well it's not enough just to believe, you must get *'in'* the elevator to get to heaven." Or the tight-roper who has just walked across Niagara Falls to the fans great applause. He gets a wheelbarrow and says, "Do you believe I can go across with this?" "Yes!" they holler back. "Then who will get *in?*" Of course leaving the impression that belief alone is not enough, but some additional subjective element is necessary.

The screaming problem with each of those illustrations is that the only "chair" or "elevator" or "wheelbarrow" which will actually get you to heaven is John 3:16 (and all the Gospel verses like it)! The only way to get "in" *that* "elevator" is by *believing*. If you believe, *then you're in!* Simple belief is the *only way* to get "in" (Jn 3:18). Whoever believes John 3:16 is true is "in" the *only* "elevator" or "wheelbarrow" or "chair" that can take one to heaven. However, if one has *only* believed what the other illustrations teach, that there is some kind of necessary element *in addition* to faith, then they have not believed the Gospel. They only believed in a *false* Gospel. That is, they are still trusting in something they do. They are believing a *believe and (fill-in-the-blank)* Gospel—a *works* Gospel anyway you cut it, not the "faith alone in Christ alone" Gospel of the Bible, *totally apart from works.*

Realize this as well, if one's faith for eternal life or justification before God is in anything subjective, that is, something one has to do himself, *regardless of what it is,* objective assurance is impossible. That is, I can never be sure this side of heaven if I actually, finally, met the subjective requirements—be they repentance, commitment, discipleship, or whatever. (As J. Vernon McGee liked to say, "If repentance is necessary for the reception of eternal life, how many tears do I need to cry before I can know for sure that I'm going to heaven?")

One writer of this Lordship salvation ilk said, "The act of placing faith into Christ must imply submission to Him—or else it could not be said that 'in Christ' was one's trust fully reposed." This is self-defeating by its own definition since it unavoidably leads to putting a certain amount of trust in one's own *submission,* and therefore the "faith" is *not* "fully reposed" in Christ!

Rather, our faith must rest in something finished and perfect to have objective assurance. Namely the finished work of Christ on our behalf, or the simple promise that "whoever believes has everlasting life." Rather than helping assurance, introspecting or looking at our works will tend to make us doubt if anything. The eyes of faith look outward, to Christ and to His work. It is unwise to get caught up in "spiritual naval gazing." Introspection even of our own faith can become a tiring rabbit trail, as if we were trying to have "faith in our faith." It is the *object* of our faith that saves us. The faith that appropriates God's gift is simple, uncomplicated, and only as good as the object in which it is placed.

"Faith comes by hearing the Word of God" (Rom 10:17). If you are lacking faith, or assurance, or if you have never believed Christ for the gift of eternal life, read John's Gospel, "The Gospel of Belief." Ask the Lord to give you an open mind and heart as you do. Untold millions have had their hearts quieted with the self-authenticating assurances of that miraculous book.

Group Questions:

1. Name some everyday occurrences where you use faith.

2. Can you give a good definition of faith?

3. How is faith "in accordance" with grace?

4. What is a reason that God has chosen to save us by *faith*?

5. Discuss this statement: "If you believe Christ at His Word, that 'whoever believes in Him has eternal life' (Jn 6:47), then you know you have eternal life. If you don't know you have eternal life, you're not believing it." Can you explain that?

14

Substitution

(Suggested Reading, Romans 5)

> *"While we were still helpless, at the right time*
> *Christ died for the ungodly.*
> *One will hardly die for a righteous man;*
> *though perhaps for the good man someone would dare even to die.*
> *But God demonstrates His own love toward us,*
> *in that while we were yet sinners, Christ died for us."*
> Romans 5:6-8

The hinge that pivots us into the next section is 5:9-10. As one might expect from a good preacher, Paul saves his best for last, and his last words of this section, 5:6-8, live up to the billing. Until now we have talked about justification, redemption, propitiation (and later reconciliation). Great words all, in *soteriology*, the study of salvation. . .

But mark it well, there is no being "declared righteous," no being "ransomed and freed," no "payment-in-full for sins," no "breaking down of the barrier" between us and God without this: *Christ dying as our Substitute in our place.*

Christ's substitutionary death is the *sine qua non* of salvation. Without it there is nothing.

The central and crucial element of Christ's death is that it was a *substitution*. The New Testament words used for Christ dying *"for"* us (*hypēr* and *anti*) have this at their forefront. In ancient papyri when someone was writing on behalf of another, perhaps an illiterate, or someone who couldn't see to write, he wrote *for*—*hyper*—that person, *in his stead, on his behalf*. However, the preposition *anti,* while translated "for," strictly and solely means "for" in the sense of *substitute*: "Archelaus was reigning *instead* (*anti*) of his father Herod…" (Mt 2:22); "…will he give him a serpent *instead* (*anti*) of a fish?" (Lk 11:11); "…an eye *for* (*anti*) an eye and a tooth *for* a tooth." *Anti* means *in the stead of,* or *in the place of*—and that's *all* it means. Christ died *for* us—*hyper* and *anti*—and substitution is the key thing to understand about it.

He died the death you and I deserved—*in our place… in our stead… on our behalf.*

… "A ransom *for* (*anti*—*in the place of*) many…" (Mt 20:28; Mk 10:45); "who gave Himself a ransom *for* (*hyper*) all" (I Tim 2:6); "who gave himself *for* us that He might redeem us" (Titus 2:14); … "For Christ also suffered once *for* sins, the Just *for* the unjust, that he might bring us to God" (I Pt 3:18). If this doesn't move you, would you pause, pray, and meditate a moment? We are at the core of the Gospel.

Please do a drill. Look at the verse at the top of the page beginning this chapter, Romans 5:6-8. Read it aloud and each time you come to the word *"for"* substitute *"in the place of."* Read it a couple of times this way, *slowly*. Let it sink in. Now, turn to Isaiah 53, a prophecy about the Suffering Servant, written seven hundred years before Christ (verified by the

Dead Sea Scrolls). Again, read Isaiah 53:4-6. Each time you read the word "our" or "we" make it very emphatic. Do so two or three times; let this idea of Christ being our Substitute get inside of you. "The Lord has laid *on Him* the iniquity of us all" (Is 53:6). This is the meaning of the *Passion of the Christ.* May it move us as it should. *(For some other substitution passages, see endnote "3").*

Personal Reflection:

Who would you die for? Probably you are thinking of relatively "good" people? Would you die for a rotten person? Saddam? Osama? Hitler? . . .Contemplate God's love, in that Christ died for us when we were "ungodly... sinners," or that he died for people who still reject and possibly still hate Him.

Further Thoughts:

I am no art connoisseur. However back in the mid-seventies I read a book by Francis Schaeffer, *How Should We Then Live?* He discussed art quite a bit, contrasting the Reformation with the Renaissance. One of the oils calls attention to was *The Raising of The Cross* by Rembrandt. Rembrandt painted many self-portraits over the course of his life. The dates are given to the works so you can progress the change as he grew from young to old. In this work, c. 1633, Rembrandt was at his usual greatness with that unique style of darkness, shade and shadow, and the beautiful, cozy, warm light attracting attention to his main object. The light's object conveyed his message. The light is on Christ, stretched and nailed on the cross as it is being hoisted into place. The light reflects off the helmet and back of a Roman soldier, pulling, straining to get the pole in its place.

While the major light is on Christ, it is also directly on the face of a helper, furrowed in concentration to put the cross in place. What is obvious is that he is wearing a painter's beret... and clothes from the 17th century. What is more obvious is that Rembrandt has painted another eerily accurate self-portrait—*himself* helping to crucify Jesus.

A dimmer light is on a person of royalty to the side, handing the sword to a soldier one presumes. However there is no soldier. Rather this person, be it Pilate, Herod or Caiaphas, is looking straight at *you*. As if he's looking directly into the lens of your camera, his eyeballs are laser-locked on yours. He's handing the sword to *you*. . . and to *me!*

What is Rembrandt's point? Yes, Herod and Pilate, the Gentiles, Romans and Jews were all complicit. But ultimately it was *our* sins that put Him on the cross. Yours and mine.

On the other hand, none of us *made* Him go to the cross, "No one takes it (My life) from me, but I lay it down of Myself (voluntarily)" (Jn 10:18). This substitutionary death was prophesied fourteen hundred years before in the Law, one thousand years before in Psalms (22), seven hundred years before in Isaiah (53), "Him being delivered up by the determined purpose and foreknowledge of God," (Ac 2:23), "foreordained before the foundation of the world" (I Pt 1:20), Christ is the substitutionary, sacrificial "Lamb slain from the foundation of the world" (Rev 13:8).

He died in our place. It was our sins that put Him there. That's why He died. He planned it from the foundation of the world, and He did it voluntarily.

Group Questions:

1. Have you ever had someone substitute for you? Have you subbed for someone?

2. If you were the only person who ever lived, do you think Christ would have died for you? Why?

3. Why is His substitutionary death the *sine qua non*, without which nothing, of salvation?

Section III

Romans 5:1–8:39

Much More Good News: Victory!

"There is therefore now no condemnation
for those who are in Christ Jesus,
who do not walk according to the flesh, but
according to the Spirit."

Romans 8:1

15

A "Much More" Salvation
(Suggested Reading, Romans 5)

"Much more then, having now been justified by His blood,
we shall be saved from wrath through Him.
For if while we were enemies we were reconciled to God
through the death of His Son,
much more, having been reconciled,
we shall be saved (from the wrath) by His life"
Romans 5:9-10

In both verses, Romans 5:9-10, *justification* and *reconciliation* are based on Christ's *death*, or "blood" ("reconciliation" is the process of enemies becoming friends). In both verses, Paul talks about a "salvation" that is "much more," *much more* he repeats, than just *justification* and *reconciliation*. After all, if it were "salvation" in how we normally think of it (i.e., salvation from hell), it would be terribly redundant. It would be nothing more than the *justification/reconciliation* just mentioned, not "much more" at all! What kind of "salvation" is Paul talking about that is so *much more*?

In both verses, unlike the justification or reconciliation[4]— *both* based on His *death*, the "salvation" to which he refers here is based on His *life*. Further, in 5:9 he specifically states that this salvation is in reference to being "saved *from wrath* through Him" (5:10 has an *ellipsis*, a common practice in the Greek text of leaving out words which are to be understood, and sometimes for emphasis. "Wrath" is the unmentioned but understood object in 5:10). If this were just a statement about being saved from the wrath of hell, how is that more than justification? Yet this *salvation* is *much more* than just that.

In the Greek text, wrath (*orgēs*) has an article with it (*tēs orgēs*), *the* wrath. This is known as an *article of previous reference* pointing back to *the wrath* he mentioned at the very beginning, the *present tense wrath* of God "which *is* (presently) revealed against all unrighteousness and ungodliness of men who suppress the truth in unrighteousness" (1:18). The "salvation" in the book of Romans, as we mentioned in the beginning, is *much more* than just salvation from hell or God's "final" wrath; it is also from the *present aspects* of God's wrath *here and now*—especially the attendant consequences of our ungodly, unrighteous choices.

These verses form a hinge around which we pivot from the section on justification into the next section on sanctification, or the "Christian life." This understanding is a key to unlocking the life-giving words to follow.[5] Rather than a cold, static interpretation (which is inevitable if the "salvation" is little more than justification), the remainder of the book will be warm, vital, motivating and filled with life-changing, life-experiencing truth.[6]

Romans 5:1, *"Therefore having been justified by faith...,"* tells us know that we are leaving the section on justification. In 5:2-5 Paul gives an introduction for the information to come in the section. It also provides an *inclusio* to mark the end of the section in Romans 8:16-39 (*inclusio* is the literary device of repeating key words or thoughts at the beginning and ending of a section, like bookends, denoting where it starts and stops). . . "[Now] we have obtained our introduction by faith into this grace in which we stand; and we exult with hope in the glory of God. And...we exult in tribulation..." This *tribulation*, or trouble, is designed by God ultimately to produce "proven character; and proven character, hope; and hope does not disappoint because the love of God has been poured out within our hearts through the Holy Spirit who was given to us" (5:2-5). These terms—*grace, glory, tribulation, proven character, hope, love* and the *Holy Spirit*—are pregnant with meaning as Paul unfolds them to us in this section, in particular at the climactic close, 8:17-39, where they come together again to complete his thought.

Personal Reflection:

Do you think there are many believers who stop at justification, and fail to go on into the "Christian life" section of life—the "much more salvation" from present wrath?

Further Thoughts:

"Justification" is from the *penalty* of sin (ch's. 2–5); "salvation" is from the *power* of sin (ch's. 6–8). Justification deals with the *legal guilt* of sin; salvation the *lethal grip* of sin. Justification, as mentioned, is through Christ's *death*. This *much more* salvation is through His *life*. That is, as Paul will explain in chapters 6–8, victory over sin and salvation from the present wrath is accomplished by Christ's resurrected life and our likewise "newness of life" in Him. We died with Christ through His death, now "we *live* with Christ" through His *life* (6:8). Now we are "dead indeed to sin but *alive to God in Christ Jesus our Lord*" (6:11). Paul will talk about this "Spirit of life in Christ" (8:2) as he explains this *much more salvation.* Christ interceding for us in heaven (8:34) and the Spirit doing so in our hearts (8:26-27) is another necessary way that *His life* dynamically saves us from the present wrath.

A believer who is living according to the Spirit is a walking miracle. "If the Spirit of Him who raised Jesus from the dead dwells in you, He who raised Christ from the dead *will also give life* to your mortal bodies through His Spirit who dwells in you" (8:11). When "by the Spirit" we "put to death the deeds of the body," *we will live*, that is, we will be *experiencing His life* within us (8:13). Paul will say the same thing to the Galatians, "I have been crucified with Christ; it is no longer I who live, but *Christ lives in me*; and the life which I now live in the flesh I live by faith in the Son of God who loved me and delivered Himself up for me" (Gal 2:20). His *death* justifies us; His *life* delivers us.

Like justification, this salvation must be acted upon by faith. "The righteousness of God is revealed from *faith* to *faith*" (justification is by faith; salvation from present wrath is also by faith), "as it is written, 'The *just* shall *live* by faith'" (1:17). Once *"just,"* (viz. "justified by faith"), the *justified* person can *experience* the new life he has in Christ *by faith*— "The just shall *live* by faith."

Justification, made available for us by His death, is appropriated by faith. Once believed, justification is past tense, "*having been justified*" (technically "past-perfect" tense, see 5:1 also). *Salvation* from the *present wrath* of God, made available through His dynamic, resurrected *life*, is also engaged by faith. As we live by faith, salvation from present wrath is what follows, *"shall be saved* from the wrath" (a "logical future" tense). Ahead, we'll see how this "living by faith" is spelled out.

On the next pages Paul will take us on a "Roman Road" journey of this salvation from the present wrath, and finally in chapter 8 to its destination.

Group Questions:

1. J. Vernon McGee likes to describe *kindness* as your mother giving you a piece of toast; *lovingkindness* is when she gives you toast with *jelly on it!* As wonderful as justification is, how is this salvation in 5:9ff. "much more" than justification?

2. Justification and reconciliation put me in right standing with God, but neither, in and of themselves, delivers me from God's present wrath. Can you explain that?

3. Justification and reconciliation are "past tense" for the believer and are both based on Christ's death. "Salvation" from the "wrath," is based on His life. What are we proposing by pointing this out?

16

Dead, Buried, and Risen
(Suggested Reading, Romans 6)

> *"Therefore we have been buried with Him through baptism*
> *into His death,*
> *in order that as Christ was raised from the dead*
> *through the glory of the Father,*
> *so we too might walk in newness of life."*
> Romans 6:4

I was a tremendous Dallas Cowboys fan growing up. Tom Landry is still one of my biggest heroes. We were blessed to have so many "victorious" seasons under him. Twenty straight to be exact. Part of his winning "formula" was, "God first, family second, football third." Some of his players thought he must have mistakenly said them in reverse order! I wish he had a formula, though, where he could have won the Super Bowl *every year.*

Lombardi was an early nemesis to Landry. He didn't win the championship every year either, but he had a formula, *KISS,* *"Keep It Simple Stupid."* The "formula" of the next readings is a sure fire way to victorious Christian living ("In all these things we are super-victors *[hypernikōmen]* through Him who loved us," Romans 8:37). It begins with these "ABC's" of Romans 6.

There's only one way to live life as God intended, *victoriously*. There's only one way to live the victorious life—*by grace*. "Much more those who receive the *abundance of grace* and of the gift of righteousness will *reign in life*...through Jesus Christ" (5:17). "*Sin shall not be master over you,* for you are not under the law, but under *grace*" (6:14).

A legalistic approach won't work. The law was not given to save us or to sanctify us. Paul goes on, "The law came in that transgression might increase" (6:20). "Through the law comes the knowledge of sin" (3:20). The law was a "tutor" to lead us to Christ by showing us our sins and need for a Savior, "that we might be justified by faith. But once faith has come, *we are no longer under a tutor!*" (Gal 3:24-25).[7]

"So, if I'm saved purely by grace, no longer under the law, why don't I live it up, sin all I want?" That's a good question. Paul responds emphatically, "May it never be!" Just as justification is by faith, so is the Christian life *lived* by faith, "*from faith to faith*, as it is written, 'The just shall *live* by faith'" (1:17). Once justified, don't stop there. Live your life by faith! *Living by faith* begins with these ABC's.

"How shall we who died to sin still live in it?" (6:2). In 6:3-11 he takes pains to make it clear that we have been united with Christ in His death, we were "*crucified*" and "*buried*" with Him. We have "*died* to sin," but we have also been "*raised* from the dead... to walk in *newness of life*" (6:4—notice, all past tenses; they are done; now they are to be *believed*).[8] You need to *believe* that the old you has died, and now you are a "new you," a new, resurrected person. Paul will show how this will be experienced and become real to us in chapter eight.

We trusted Christ concerning His *death* in the justification phase—that His death made full and final payment for our sins. Now we trust Him for His *life* in the living it out phase. His resurrected life within us, energized by the dynamic working of the Holy Spirit, will give life to our mortal bodies and enable us to "put to death" the sinful deeds of the body. When we act upon this in *faith*, then we will really *live!* Not just possessing eternal life, but experiencing it right now in all of its victory, joy, peace and hope (see Rom 8:10-13 for a preview).

We are now to "consider ourselves dead to sin, but alive to God in Christ Jesus," (the first command in Romans) and to "present" our new, risen selves—every part of us—to God (6:11-13). We are not to "let sin reign" in our "mortal body," a "body of death" as Paul calls it (7:24). But how? How can we keep sin from being master over us? Paul will unfold it bit by bit. But it begins with these preliminary understandings— crucified, died, buried, raised—"so that we might walk in newness of life." Let's find out how to make this resurrected "newness of life" an experienced reality.

Personal Reflection:

"For he who has died has been freed from sin" (6:7). Would you say that before faith in Christ, sin was your "master?" If so, in what way?

Further Thoughts:

Have you ever been to the Holy Land? Were you there two thousand years ago? Do you remember the song, "*Were You*

There?"— "Were you there when they crucified my Lord? Were you there when they laid Him in the tomb? Were you there when He rose up from the grave?. . ." You may think I'm crazy, but somehow, when you believed in Christ, you "*were baptized* into Christ" and you were "baptized into His *death*" (6:3)—and you *were* there!

He is not talking about water baptism here, which is *ritual* baptism "into His *name*." He is talking about Spirit baptism, *real* baptism "into *Christ*." Through this baptism Paul says we "were crucified with Him" (6:6), "buried" and "raised" (6:4). You didn't do any of this, it was done for you. These verbs are in the passive voice. You might can kill yourself, but you can't crucify yourself. You could nail one nail in, maybe two, but how would you do the others? If you're dead, you certainly can't bury yourself, and you sure as heck can't raise yourself! God did all this for you. It's done. You might have never been to Golgotha or seen the Garden Tomb, but somehow, in the miracle of Spirit baptism, every believer was there. You have to take it on faith.

These truths that we believe—that we have been crucified, buried and raised with Christ—have implications. In fact the first command of Romans 6:11, comes on the heels of these truths, followed by three other commands. Two things to do and two things to deny.

First, "Likewise you also, *reckon* (imperative of *logizomai*, same word in 4:5-6, *count on it*,) yourselves to be dead to sin, but alive to God in Christ Jesus our Lord." Second, "Therefore *do not let* sin *reign* in your mortal body, that you should obey its lusts." Third, "And *do not present* your members as instruments of unrighteousness to sin," (fourth) "but *present* yourselves to God as being alive from the dead, and your members as instruments of righteousness to God."

If the Christian life section of Romans stopped here, it wouldn't be much different than the old law—a bunch of commands and no power to keep them. But it doesn't stop. Please keep reading for Paul is going to show us God's supernatural power for keeping these commands and how this will come alive with meaning in chapter eight. Then we won't just believe facts about the resurrection life and our death to sin, he'll show us how to *experience* resurrection power here and now. He's whetting our appetite with these ABC's...

Group Questions:

1. What do you think the intent is going to be in the unfolding of the section, that we are "dead to sin?" So what?

2. What is the intent, at this beginning stage, of him telling us that we are raised with Christ? So what?

3. "*Presenting* ourselves"—every part of us (our members) to God "as being alive from the dead?" What is that going to mean? If you do so, what would you expect God to do with it?

4. Paul will expound later on the how-to part of "walking in newness of life." For now, what thoughts come to your mind with this expression?

17

Freedom, Fruitfulness and Failure

"And having been set free from sin,
you became slaves of righteousness...
What fruit did you have then
in the things for which you are now ashamed?
For the end of those things is death."
Romans 6:18, 21

Before addressing the problem of our new resurrected self, housed in a dead body, where also resides a foreign alien named Sin, there are a couple of things Paul wants to address. First, that we are free. He repeats that we are not to continue in sin just because we are under grace and not under the law (6:15). Believers who do so will reap what they sow—shame, and the present wrathful consequences connected to their sin (6:21, cf. 1:18-32). Though free to sin, there are serious consequences. Through the Gospel, something is new. Now we are free *not* to sin.

One of the very first lessons for us "saved sinners" is to learn that we don't *have to sin* any more. We've been *set free!* "Set free" from the addictive, compulsive nature of sin, something we were enslaved to before grace, "Having been *set free from sin,* you became slaves of righteousness" (6:18). Paul will flesh this out in our next readings and show us how it works practically, but for now count on it: You're free. You don't *have to* sin anymore.[9]

Secondly, we have died to the law that we might be married to Christ (7:4). Referring to when we were "slaves to sin" Paul asks, "What *fruit* did you have then in the things for which you are now ashamed? For the end of those things is *death*" (6:21). While sin is "pleasurable for a season," its *fruit* is bitter. When he says the "end of those things is *death*," he could have in mind the physical death that results from any sin left unchecked. James talked about this, "When lust has conceived it gives birth to sin; and sin, when it is full grown, brings forth ("births") *death*" (Jas 1:15). The progeny of sinful desire and sin, ultimately, is physical death. "When we were in the flesh," Paul employs the same imagery as James, "the sinful passions which were aroused by the law were at work in our members to *bear fruit to death*" (Rom 7:5). Paul says our old self has died and therefore is free from our old "husband" the *law*. Now, married to *Christ*, we are to have *offspring* of a different sort, we are to "*bear fruit* to God" (Rom 7:6).

But there is another kind of death at the forefront of Paul's mind. Namely, the death-type spiritual and psychological experience, *even for believers*, that occurs when we sin. The "fruit to death" which we bore when we were in the flesh can still be our offspring if we walk after the flesh. The guilt, condemnation, shame, worry, frustration, depression... the "wretchedness," or "miserableness," as Paul describes it, are all part of the *fruit to death* that even believers might experience when they sin. All part and parcel of the present tense wrath of God, spoken of by Paul at the beginning (1:18-32). "Receiving in their own persons the due penalty of their error" (1:27) is part of the death-type "fruit" Paul has in mind, the present wrath from which God wants to deliver us!

As we'll see, Paul himself was not immune from the fruits of his failures. Even an Apostle is not beyond living in the flesh, and insofar as Paul did, he was "miserable," "confused," and "condemned" to bearing the bitter consequences. Let's look at his story in the next reading, discover his success, and follow his pattern.

Personal Reflection:

Do you really believe that you're set free from sin? Is there a sin in your life that you have trouble shaking?

Further Thoughts:

Before faith in Christ we were "slaves to sin" (6:6, 17-20). It was our master, our captain and commander.

After WWII some of the key Nazi members awaited their trial at the International Military Tribunal in Nürnberg. One of them was Reichsmarshall Hermann Göring. He was not only head of the Luftwaffe, he was the second-ranking Nazi leader next to Hitler. This phenomenon might have happened on several occasions at different locales, but I remember watching a WWII documentary when a former German soldier was talking about it happening to him. Göring, while waiting for his trial and even after the sentencing (in which he was found guilty of all counts), though imprisoned, held the German soldiers in sway. Those that surrounded him trembled in fear. Even though he was deposed, they would have carried out his orders anyway. In fact one of them doing so gave him a poison pill so Göring could avoid the gallows.

Similarly with us, Christ has "condemned sin in the flesh"—pronounced its sentence (8:3) All that remains for us is to, by the Spirit, *execute* the death penalty upon it which Christ has decreed (see 8:3b and 8:13). Nevertheless, "old habits die hard." For some of us, we were enslaved for a long time under sin. It was a long lifestyle of obeying his commands. Though he is deposed, jailed (awaiting sentence) and has no more authority over us, we far too often bring ourselves back under the sway of "old man sin."

Group Questions:

1. Why are believers not to continue in sin... they are already "justified," so why shouldn't they "sin it up?"

2. Think of some believers—without mentioning names—who, though under grace, carelessly continued sinning? What has been the result?

3. When one weighs both the "benefits" and consequences of sin, is it worth it? Someone has well-said that had David considered the outcome of his sin with Bathsheba —especially had he been allowed to experience just *some* of the bitter consequences that resulted—and then asked himself whether it would be "worth it," there is no way he would have committed the sin! (see 2 Sam 12:10-14). Would anyone like to share a modern-day story where the "fruits" of sin simply were not worth it?

18

Possessing Eternal Life, But Experiencing Death (Suggested Reading, Romans 7)

"For sin...killed me... (The law is holy and good.
Has then what is good become death to me? Certainly not!
But sin, that it might appear sin, was producing death in me
through what is good)... For the law is spiritual, but I am carnal. . .
For what I am doing, I do not understand. For what I will to do,
that I do not practice; but what I hate, that I do.
If, then, I do what I will not to do, I agree with the law that it is good.
But now, it is no longer I who do it, but sin that dwells in me.
For I know that in me (that is in my flesh) nothing good dwells;
for to will is present with me,
but how to perform what is good I do not find.
For the good that I will to do, I do not do;
but the evil I will not to do, that I practice.
Now if I do what I will not to do, it is no longer I who do it,
but sin that dwells in me.
I find then a law, that evil is present with me,
the one who wills to do good.
For I delight in the law of God according to the inward man.
But I see another law in my members,
warring against the law of my mind,
and bringing me into captivity to the law of sin which is in my members.
O wretched man that I am!
Who will deliver me from this body of death?" Romans 7:11-24

"**S**in...killed me," said Paul. And it kills us. Not just physically, but emotionally, psychologically and in a spiritual kind of way. For a believer, sin causes confusion (7:15). It causes self-loathing (7:15) and all sorts of internal conflict (7:23). Sin causes a feeling of "wretchedness" (misery, despair). Paul is painting a perfect portrait of a believer who possesses eternal life, but is experiencing "death."

In humility he shows his humanness by identifying with something most grace believing Christians have gone through at some point. The frustration and failure of trying to live the Christian life in our own self-effort, however well-intentioned. Whatever the case, mark it well, it is not just a matter of trying harder!

The Christian life is not a matter of living in our own "will power"—even though regenerate! In fact, what Paul "wills to do" he does not, and what he "wills not to do," he does! Not only is the result confusing, conflicting and self-condemning, it ends in despair and a sort of spiritual death. *"Sin killed me... sin was producing death in me..."* Certainly, no believer can lose eternal life (Jn 3:16; 5:24). After all, it's *eternal*, and if it wasn't, Christ should have called it something else! But a child of God can experience a "death" type experience when he sins—the guilt, shame, misery and perhaps feeling of "death." "Who will deliver me from this body of death!?" Where is that *much more* salvation "deliverance?" The answer is in Romans 8:1-14, our next reading.

Personal Reflection:

1. Would you say you experience more life or death? Why?

2. Have you had this feeling of "wretchedness,"
   miserableness, because of sin? What was it like?

Further Thoughts:

"You're killing me Smalls!" Do you remember that famous line from the movie, *Sandlot?* Maybe you have become exacerbated trying to explain something to a friend and he's just not getting it, "You're killing me," you might say. There are more "deaths" one can die than the one where we actually stop breathing.

Sin was killing Paul. In fact, he goes on to describe an experience, or a montage of experiences, where sin "killed" him. Not physically, but the kind of spiritual/psychological death one feels from extreme frustration or failure, guilt and shame, confusion and chaos, despair and depression, self-loathing, and things of this sort. Feelings, coincidentally, that often go with sin. Whether a believer or not, those feelings are part of the human record. In fact, believers—when they sin—should be more prone, by virtue of what they believe and their new nature, to feeling these painful, bitter "fruits" of sin.

We have already seen that we were "set free" from sin (6:7, 18, etc.), but we can be suckered back into "captivity" to it as well (7:23). In our freedom, we don't *have to* present ourselves to God (though we *should*); we can *re*-present ourselves to sin and come under its bondage again (6:16). "*Whoever*," Christian or not, Jesus said, "*Whoever* commits sin is a slave to sin" (Jn 8:34). And Paul said, "the wages of sin is death" (6:23). We use that as an evangelistic verse, and it is fine to do so since it is speaking a general truth, but be aware that it is in the middle of the *Christian life* portion of Romans! The warning is foremost to Christians, "the *wages* of sin," its bitter *results*, is "death."

Lowering the "minimum wage" of sin is not an option. We need deliverance from sin. I hope you can't wait for the answer. Why not turn the page and find out now.

Group Questions:

1. In what ways did sin "kill" Paul? In what ways have you experienced similar death-type "wages" for your sins?

2. "To will is present, but how to perform what is good is not." Why do you suppose the Christian life is not just a matter of our own willpower?

3. Paul said he was "wretched" (miserable, despairing). Would God ever want us feeling so miserable, why or why not?

4. Have you been guilty of trying to live the Christian life through will-power and self-effort? How did it work for you?

19

Victory!
(Suggested Reading, Romans 8)

"There is therefore now no condemnation
to those who are in Christ Jesus,
who do not walk according to the flesh but according to the Spirit.
For the law of the Spirit of life in Christ Jesus has made me free
from the law of sin and death...
that the righteous requirement of the law might be fulfilled in us
who do not walk according to the flesh
but according to the Spirit"
Romans 8:1-2, 4

This is the crowning point of the "much more" salvation of Romans. How can we be delivered from this "body of death?" How can we be rescued from the "law of sin and death," ...saved from the "death" experience Paul just described of himself (7:15-25)? The answer is here.

Paul is not mindlessly repeating the truth of Romans 1–5 when he says "there is no *condemnation* in Christ Jesus." The word condemnation is not the normal word for condemnation (as if a final judgment) which is *krima* the *pronounced* judgment (cf. Lk 23:40; I Cor 11:34; Jas 3:1); or, *krisis*, the *process* of judgment, (Jn 3:19, 5:24; Jas 5:12). The word Paul selects fits perfectly with our interpretation, *katakrima*, the *penalty* of judgment, the penal servitude that is a result of judgment.[10]

The first phase of victory from the punishing consequences of God's present wrath, this *katakrima* condemnation, such as Paul has just described of himself (7:15-25), is to be *"in Christ"*—a technical term Paul uses for every believer. At the moment of faith, each believer is "baptized into Christ" (cf. 6:13ff.; I Cor 12:13). The second phase is realizing that, being *set free* from the law of sin and death, I don't *have to* sin. The completion phase of this salvation is for those *in Christ*, to *"not walk according to the flesh but according to the Spirit"* (8:1, 4).

In Romans 8:2 Paul repeats a truth, that we have been "made free" (same expression as in 6:18, *"set free"*). But now he says the one walking by the Spirit is not only "set free from sin" (6:18), but he is *set free* from "the *law of sin* and death." This refers to the immediately preceding verses, where Paul describes his struggle with sin as a believer insofar as he did not walk according to the Spirit: "But I see another *law* in my members, warring against the law of my mind, and bringing me into captivity to the *law of sin* which is in my members... So then, with the mind I myself serve the law of God, but with my flesh the *law of sin*" (7:23, 25). This begs the question of how to escape or overcome the *"law of sin."*

Paul is using "law" here in terms of "rule" or "principle," like the "laws of physics." The "law of sin" is a spiritual phenomena as true in life as the "law of gravity." Insofar as the believer seeks to keep the demands of God in his own self effort, the *law of sin captures* him, and with that the deathly consequences follow. It is a *law,* a *rule* of life. Paul now

103

introduces a higher law, "the law of the Spirit of life in Christ." As believers stay aware of their *newness of life in Christ* (6:4-10), and ever-presently avail themselves of the *Spirit's* enablement, "walking according to the Spirit," the believer is "set free" from the captivating "law of sin and death." In addition, "the righteous requirement of the law is fulfilled in us..." This begs a further question, how do we *walk according to the Spirit?* Let's look at that in the next reading...

Personal Reflection:

Have you noticed that the principle, "the law of sin and death," is ready to re-capture you at every turn?
Does one have to give into it? Why not?

Further Thoughts:

When I was in my freshman year of college I was reading through Romans. I was tracking along fine, except for the part in 7:13-25 where Paul—even the Apostle Paul—seems to be defeated! That's what it said. I couldn't get around it, yet even as a fairly new "student" of the Word I knew something wasn't right. "If Paul didn't have victory over sin, how was I going to have it?!" I couldn't quote chapter and verse to disprove such thinking, but there was something in my heart, no doubt from somewhere in the Bible, that said this couldn't be right. "God wouldn't just leave us hanging to be defeated, with no way out," I thought.

I was a little flustered so I prayed about it. The spring semester ended. I came home and was reading a good Christian book, unrelated to Romans. Out of the blue the author said something that has changed my life ever since. "Too many Christians leave their lives in Romans 7 and don't go on to Romans 8!" I couldn't wait to hear what he had to say. "The chapters and verses," he went on, "were put in hundreds of years later by editors." The fact is, 8:1 and following is the joyful, climactic answer to Paul's predicament in 7:13-25. I would have read it as thus had it not been separated by a huge "Chapter 8." (I'm embarrassed that I wasn't smart enough to figure this out on my own. But I'm also convinced that being a spiritual follower of Christ is not about being smart. Seeking the Lord, prayer and dependence on the Spirit, are far more important issues than intellectual acumen for understanding God's Word. I can think of a number of times where the Lord has helped me get the Biblical answers I was seeking, not because of personal mental prowess, but in obvious answer to prayer—seeing something or coming upon something that gave the answer, but which I never would have arrived at just on my own).

The writer I mentioned above also added, "The 'law of sin and death' is like the law of gravity... As certain laws of aerodynamics set a plane "free" from the law of gravity, 'the law of the Spirit of life in Christ' has *set (us) free* from the 'law of sin and death.'" That made sense to me. Attempting to fight temptation in my own self-effort, however well-intentioned, ended in failure. Added to that the troubling echo, "If *Paul* failed, who are you to think you are?" Now I saw Paul's answer in 8:1 and following! I claimed it for my own—and it worked! It wasn't just a matter of *trying*, now I saw it was also a matter of *trusting*—trusting the Lord that I didn't *have to* sin, and that His Spirit would do for me what I could not do on my own.

Group Questions:

1. What are some of the temporal "penal" consequences that you have experienced because of sin?

2. Can you share the victorious feeling in your struggle with a particular habit or sin when you realized you didn't *have to* do it anymore?

3. Can you share a victory in your life that wasn't just about trying, but about trusting, too?

20

Walking According to the Spirit

"For those who live according to the flesh
set their minds on the things of the flesh,
but those who live according to the Spirit,
the things of the Spirit.
For to be carnally minded is death,
but to be spiritually minded is life and peace...
For if you live according to the flesh you will die;
but if by the Spirit you put to death the deeds of the body, you will live."
Romans 8:5-6, 13

I want to be set free from the law of sin and death. I want to be rescued from the condemning consequences of my sins. I understand to do so I need to *"walk according to the Spirit,"* (8:4) but how do I do that?!

Paul uses the imagery of "walking" for a reason. Walking is a balancing act—just watch any toddler, or look at the rehab patient trying to relearn the art of walking. Paul made it emphatically clear that the Christian life is not a matter of our own—even though regenerate—*willpower!* ("The things I *will to do*, I do not; the things I *will not to do*, I do!" see 7:15-25). It is not a matter of just our fleshly self-efforts.

As a new, regenerated person, I make choices—in fact my new mind agrees with God and wants to do right (7:22)—I "will" to do the right things. While in and of itself that is not enough to actually *do*, or *to practice*, the right things, it is the *first step!* "Walking" *according to the Spirit* requires that "step" of the will. Now, at the same time I need help to stay "balanced" so I can take that next "step"—the step to believe God the Holy Spirit for His enabling power. Then another step of "willing" the right things—which naturally comes out of my new life in Christ—followed by another step of depending on the Lord. It's not me alone; it's not the Lord alone, it's both of us *walking together*. But it's not just about willpower and dependence on the Higher Power, it's about a *mindset...*

It is not just a "walk," it is a life, a lifestyle, of *living* according to the Spirit. If we *set our minds* on the *things of the flesh*, we are living according to the flesh, and vice versa. The same is true of the Spirit. As the next verse shows, we are dealing primarily with an orientation of our thoughts, a spiritual mindset. "(T)o be carnally *minded* is death (lit., "The *mindset* of the *flesh* is death"); but to be spiritually *minded* is life and peace" (lit., "but the *mindset* of the Spirit is life and peace").

Whether focused on fulfilling God's laws in my own fleshly effort, or consumed with the fleshly impulses of sin, such a *mindset* is *death*—e.g., the death-like, joy-killing, life-robbing experience Paul just described of himself (7:10-13, 24). A mental orientation toward the Spirit, conversely, includes *attention toward Christ* and our new life in Him (8:2). Thinking on the *things of the Spirit* also includes the truth just mentioned in 8:3 about Christ—pondering His *pattern* of life *to be imitated*, His *provision* for life (the cross) *to be contemplated*, and His *punishing* victory over sin, toward life (our ability to *experience* life), *to be actuated*. Christ's death "condemned"—pronounced judgment on—*sin in the flesh.*[12] Now, *by His Spirit,* we can carry-out that death sentence, "But if *by the Spirit you put to death* the deeds of the body [viz., *sins in the flesh]*, you will *live*" (8:13). Such a spiritual *mindset* and personally decisive (note: *"you* put to death"), *Spirit-empowered* "execution" results in the *"life and peace"* experience God intended (8:6, 13), antithetical to the death/despair experience of a fleshly mindset.

Personal Reflection:
Have you experienced "putting to death" sin, with the supernatural help of the Spirit?

Further Thoughts:
Most of us are familiar with the "Twelve-Step" program of Alcoholics Anonymous. Countless people have found sobriety through it. Each of us would do well to read the "big book," *Alcoholics Anonymous.* A friend gave it to me one time (I don't drink) because we had talked about the spiritual principles within it and because he felt it was such a wonderful read (he's not a drinker either). What impressed me are the testimonies, one after another, all saying the same thing—how they had tried, over and over, to stop drinking, but in and of themselves couldn't. Each attempt was ultimately met with failure. Not until they "called upon a Higher Power" were they able to be delivered from the terrible addiction. Even then, they unanimously confessed, it is a moment by moment dependence on the Higher Power. As Paul would say, it is not just a matter of our own willpower alone! Further, it's a "step" at a time, like walking...

Hopefully you have never, or will never, have to face such a life-destroying addiction. Part of what Paul is getting at in

Romans is that all sin is addictive. There is a "*law* of sin and death," sin "brings us into *captivity*," and "we are *slaves* to whom we obey, whether sin leading to death, or obedience leading to righteousness" (6:16; 7:23, etc.). Jesus said it simply, "Most assuredly, I say to you, whoever commits sin is a slave to sin" (Jn 8:34). All sin has an addictive element to it. It enslaves us to its consequences and seeks to enslave us to its pleasures and habits. The Good News of Romans is of a salvation where we are delivered from slavery to sin, and through His Spirit enabled to live victoriously over it. According to Romans 6–8, there is no addiction or enslavement to sin that cannot be overcome through His power. By His Spirit we can experience life, peace and victory.

Group Questions:

1. Can anyone share about a friend, relative, or yourself, who overcame addiction through depending on a Higher Power?

2. As Christians, we know the "Higher Power" is the Lord. Can any of you share about overcoming a sin or bad habit with the Lord's help?

3. Walking according to the Spirit includes both my will and dependence on the Lord's power. Why is it both?

4. Those who live according to the Spirit set their minds on the things of the Spirit; the mind set on the Spirit is life and peace. What "things" does one think on? Describe a spiritual mindset.

21

Led By The Spirit. . . Into Suffering

For if you live according to the flesh you will die;
but if by the Spirit you put to death the deeds of the body, you will live.
For as many as are led by the Spirit of God, these are sons of God. . .

We are children of God, and if children, then heirs—
heirs of God and co-heirs with Christ
if indeed we co-suffer with Him,
in order that we may also be co-glorified with Him."
Romans 8:13-14, 17

The notion that a believer cannot walk *"according to the flesh,"* or cannot "practice" sin, is as naïve as it is unbiblical. If—and when—believers walk *according to the flesh*, they'll *die*. There is a real possibility of premature death for a believer following the flesh, and certainly the reality of the "death" experience that "killed" Paul, in a manner of speaking (7:10-11ff.).

But to the believers who by the Spirit live victoriously over sin, not only will they experience *life* on the level God meant it ("you will *live*"), they are also described as being *led by the Spirit of God*. Those thus *led* are not mere children, but are mature *"sons* of God."

111

All believers are "*children of God*," begotten of Him (Jn 1:12; Jas 1:18). Since they are children, they are *heirs* (first-class condition in Greek represents matter of fact). These "children" are then "co-heirs" with Christ *if* (Gk. Third-class condition, matter of *possibility*) *if* they "co-suffer" with Him in order that they may be "co-glorified" with Him.

As you might know, in the Hebrew economy the firstborn got a double-portion of the inheritance. Lest we miss it, Paul reminds us shortly that, "Christ is the *firstborn among many brethren*" (8:29). Get this: We are all *heirs of God* by virtue of being His *children*—every believer. But we are not all *co-heirs* with the Firstborn unless we live a life like His, namely a life that involves *suffering*. Of course we cannot suffer quite like, or anywhere close to the amount, He suffered (Heb 12:3-4). However with the Spirit's enabling we can follow the pattern He set down for us which included *suffering*. *Suffering*, for example, in the very nature of resisting sin, keeping His commands, or even the involuntary suffering that is part of living in a fallen world.

It is no mistake that the *Spirit* is mentioned more in Romans 8 than in any other chapter, twenty-one times, mainly in the first half. Neither is it a mistake that the second half is about *suffering*. A *Spirit-led life* will be led into *suffering for Christ*. This latter part of Romans 8 forms an *inclusio* with 5:2-5. He ends the section with the themes he began, *hope, glory, tribulation, perseverance, character* and the *love of God* that is with us and never leaves. God wants us to be *glorified* like Christ (8:17-18). The *sufferings* necessary to get there are not worthy to be compared to the *glory* that results. "We were *saved* in this *hope* (and)...eagerly wait for it with *perseverance*" (8:24-25). God's purpose for each of us is to *conform* us to the *character* of Christ, and He works all things together—(including *sufferings* or *tribulations*)—for this ultimate "good" (Ro 8:28-29). God is for us and nothing can separate us from His *love* (8:31-39). This is the "Spirit of life in Christ" and where walking according to the Spirit leads.

Personal Reflection:

We have all suffered. Has there been a time(s) you voluntarily "suffered" for Christ?

Further Thoughts:

I was talking about this subject of suffering and rewards one day to a group of missionaries. There was an older couple there who had served the Lord for many years. They weren't won over with my idea of suffering. They had served the Lord for nearly fifty years of fulltime ministry and honestly didn't feel they had "suffered" that much. The fact is, they had "suffered" in many ways over those years, voluntarily and involuntarily. However, their walk with the Lord was so close and they were so filled with the "joy and peace in believing, abounding in hope by the power of the Holy Spirit," that suffering had not been their focus, but the Lord.

To put it another way, living according to the Spirit is primarily about having a spiritual mindset like the couple above (8:5-6). By "mindset" we mean something like this. My son came out of the womb loving baseball, so I've come to love it as a result. In the summer I go to bed thinking about it and wake-up thinking about it. Some of you are golf minded, or business minded. What do you focus on and fill your thoughts with? The spiritually minded person, according to the latter half of Romans 8, while aware of suffering, would be focusing more on the other items there. She will be thinking about co-reigning with Christ and the glory to come; on sustaining hope and perseverance (8:17-25); on the Spirit's sensitive involvement and care (26-27); on trusting that God is working all things together for her good (28-30); on His non-condemning, unconditional, never-changing love; on Christ's victory and prayers for us (31-39) and the many other wonderful, warm spiritual thoughts of the last half of chapter eight. A "spiritually minded" person will be thinking on these thoughts and the countless other good thoughts about her Lord in the Scriptures. That is to say, she wouldn't be consumed only with the topic of suffering!

We would be wise to be aware that suffering is part of life. As we mature in Christ we certainly should not think that there will be less suffering. If anything, Christ's suffering increased with age. Rather, we should seek the attitude toward trials and suffering like Paul had and what he began this section with. We "rejoice in hope of the glory of God," especially the prospect of God being glorified in our lives as they are conformed to Christ-like character. Therefore, "we also glory (exult) in tribulations, knowing that tribulation produces perseverance; and perseverance, approved character; and approved character, hope. Now hope does not disappoint, because the love of God has been poured out in our hearts by the Holy Spirit who was given to us" (Ro 5:2-5). For those living according to the Spirit, even suffering takes on a joyous, hopeful, loving tone. As our focus is on Christ and "the things of the Spirit," I would suspect, like the couple above, much of the "suffering" will hardly be noticed.

You've seen street signs and barricades with big letters, "MEN AT WORK." A spiritual person sees trials and tribulation and reads, "GOD AT WORK." He doesn't shrink back from trials and sufferings, but "exults" in them. He knows God is working in his life with a wonderful end in view. With hope in his heart for what God is going to do, and reminding himself of God's love anew, he knows "GOD IS AT WORK," and He's "*working* it all together for good!"

A spiritually minded person overcomes both sin and suffering—"In *all these things* we are more than conquerors (= we are super-victors, *hypernikōmen*) through Him who loved us" (8:37).

Group Questions:

1. It is not in human nature to welcome suffering. How is the spiritual person different?

2. Not every believer chooses to suffer voluntarily for Christ. What are some ways that a spiritually minded person might choose to "suffer" for Christ?

3. What is another reason given in this passage, besides becoming like Christ, to voluntarily suffer with Him?

4. The tenor of the Christian life is one of joy. How do you harmonize that with the fact that, at times, the Spirit will lead us to suffer?

Section IV

Romans 9–16

Good News: Summary

"I beseech you therefore, brethren,
by the mercies of God,
that you present your bodies a living sacrifice,
holy, acceptable to God,
which is your reasonable service.
And do not be conformed to this world,
but be transformed
by the renewing of your mind,
that you may prove what is that good and
acceptable and perfect will of God."

Romans 12:1-2

22

Preface to Romans 9–11
(Suggested Reading, Romans 9)

Compatibility of Divine Foreknowledge and Human Freedom[13]

My favorite C.S. Lewis book is *The Great Divorce*. It is a fictional bus ride from hell to heaven with the fascinating stories of why so many of the people from hell want to catch the next bus back. It becomes a treatise on man's freewill and God's sovereignty. C.S. Lewis gets on board and upon arrival in heaven a tour guide has been assigned to him. It's George MacDonald.[14] As they go on the tour together, MacDonald explains various things. Lewis asks his host, "But what about the ghosts who never get on the omnibus (to heaven) at all?" "Everyone who wishes does," comes the reply, "Never fear. There are only two kinds of people in the end: those who say to God, 'Thy will be done,' and those to whom God says, in the end, '*Thy* will be done.' All that are in Hell choose it. Without that self-choice there could be no Hell…"[15]

"Every one who wishes does," is tantamount to the Scripture, "Whosoever will may come…" (Rev 22:17), or "Whosoever believeth in Him should not perish…" (Jn 3:16), or a verse that Lewis says fit his personal case, "If any man is willing to do his will, he shall know of the doctrine" (Jn 7:17).

To say the Bible does not teach freewill is so blatantly off the mark as to be shameful. The Bible's *commands* imply freewill, its *judgments* demand it (How can God rightly judge us if people only do what they were programmed to do, as if they were automatons or robots?). The word "will" is itself frequently used throughout the Bible, "O Jerusalem, Jerusalem, the city that kills the prophets and stones those who are sent to her! How I *longed* (*thelō*, "willed") to gather you as a hen gathers her chicks, but you were *unwilling* (*athelō*, Mt 23:37); "Whoever desires ("wills", *thelō*) let him take of the water of life freely." There are commands to make *choices*, "Choose you this day..." Those denying that the Bible presupposes freewill are simply imposing their philosophy onto it.

Freewill is the teaching that at any given time we could have chosen otherwise than what we chose. *Fatalism* is the philosophy that we don't have freewill. Islam is fatalistic; Christianity is not. *Determinism* is a philosophy that says we have no freewill; our choices are pre-determined by other forces.[16] Hard-Calvinism is fatalistic. Calvinism adopts a philosophy (that we don't have freewill), then sees the Bible through those glasses. One would hardly have arrived at such fatalistic conclusions simply reading the Bible alone. Almost certainly exposure to philosophy or teaching along those lines entered somewhere. The Bible obviously teaches both the freewill of man and the sovereignty of God! While a mystery, like other theological doctrines, it is not a contradiction. God's sovereignty includes man's freewill.[17] Hard-Calvinism, denying freewill, does away with the mystery. In the end, Calvinism is philosophical determinism cloaked in the sheep's clothing of Biblical language.

Romans 9 is the main passage used by hard-Calvinists to "prove" that we do not have freewill. One can see how a simple reading of it could draw fatalistic conclusions—if we read virtually no other parts of the Bible (which affirm and infer freewill throughout). This is the warning of 2 Peter 1:20, that *"no Scripture is a matter of its own interpretation."*

One of the earliest and best teachings I got in my Christian walk in fact came from a hard-Calvinist, *"Scriptura ex scriptura explicanda est."* Scripture is explained out of other Scripture. Scripture is to be understood in light of other Scripture. (Unfortunately this dear gentleman did not practice what he preached, letting his theology inform his Bible and not vice versa). What we want to warn against is an overly simplistic view of Romans 9 which does not take other parts of the Divine record into account. We also want to warn against a view that makes God not so much be the Author of our salvation as the Author of our sin, a blasphemous thought, but one to which hard-Calvinism inevitably leads.[18]

Personal Reflection:

What do you think about Lewis' line that there are only two kinds of people in the world in the end? Where are you?

Group Questions:

1. Do you believe in freewill? Why or Why not?

2. Do you believe the Gospel is a "whosoever will…" proposition? If not, why not?

3. Have you ever thought of God as the Author of sin, or that He made you sin?

4. Why is it important not to interpret a Scripture in "isolation," i.e., without bringing other Scriptures to bear?

23

Prognostication
(Suggested Reading, Romans 10-11)

> *"For I do not desire, brethren,*
> *that you should be ignorant of this mystery,*
> *lest you should be wise in your own estimation,*
> *that blindness in part has happened to Israel*
> *until the fullness of the Gentiles has come in."*
> Romans 11:25

D o you ever watch college or NFL pre-game reports. It is good entertainment just for the sake of seeing how far off their prognostications can be. Their forecasts, or *foreknowledge*, is often quite lacking. God's isn't. Romans 9–11 is a sweeping panorama of God's salvation history, beginning with Christ and coming to our day.

Maybe you've heard about the fellow who stubbornly kept asking this girl out. Finally she gave him the basis for her refusals, "I would not have you, ignorant brethren!" (1:13). Nor does God want us *ignorant* (*agnoein*, from the word we get agnostic) about what He's up to with Israel and the Gentiles.

A temporary *blindness* has occurred on the nation Israel *until the fullness of the Gentiles*. Of course, not every Jew will be blinded during this period. There will still be a *remnant*, more than a few from Israel—Paul himself being one—who will believe during this time (11:4-5). In the meantime the larger part of Israel, in her *blindness*, will *stumble* over the *stumbling stone*.

Pursuing a "law of righteousness" they did not attain it because, "they did not seek it by faith, but as it were, by works of the law." Many Gentiles on the other hand, "who did not pursue righteousness, *have attained* righteousness, even the *righteousness of faith*" (9:30-33). Paul expounds on this, "For they (non-believing Israel) being *ignorant* of God's righteousness, and seeking to establish their own righteousness, have not submitted to the righteousness of God. For Christ is the end of the law for righteousness to everyone who believes" (Rom 10:3-4; Phil 3:10). Once the "fullness of the Gentiles" have come to faith (been grafted in) there will be an awakening of Israel to faith (11:11-32).

The *stumbling stone*, or "block" (9:33; 11:9), over which Israel stumbled, is the *faith-in-Christ* principle for righteousness as opposed to the *works-principle* for righteousness they supposed. As mentioned in the first section, only the former imparts righteousness, the latter never could. God has ordained from their stumble "to provoke (Israel) to jealousy," since "salvation has come to the Gentiles" (11:11). A vivid example that God doesn't just zap some with salvation and not others. More complicated than that, He wants us all to be saved (I Tim 2:4) and employs many various means to do so, even jealousy or envy.

Paul uses the language of appearance. God did not *make* Israel *fall* so as to give *riches to the Gentiles* (11:12), nor *actually* "*cast them away* to reconcile the world" (11:15; In fact in 11:1 He says absolutely that God has *not* "cast away His people.").

During this time of Israel's unbelief (and the Gentiles' coming to faith) it can be *figuratively said* that He "*cast them away* to reconcile the world." He obviously didn't pick them up like a literal piece of trash and throw them in a huge Tidy Dumpster. It could "appear" to us looking on that God "cast them away;" but mark it well, the state of non-believing Israel is also a *willful* state *on their part*.[19]

God wants them to be saved ("who desires *all men* to be saved") and is actively pursuing them. But because of *their* will in rejecting Christ, it *appears* God has "cast them away." (Remember: Part of God's wrath is the outworking of the consequences of *our* choices, 1:18-32). "All day long I have stretched out My hand to a disobedient and contrary people" (10:21)—He always seeks them, though *figuratively* it looks like He *cast them away*.

That "God has given them… *eyes that they should not see, and ears that they should not hear*" or "that *blindness* in part has happened to Israel," again is the heavily figurative language of appearance. It is not as though God has chosen from eternity to zap them so, try as they might, to see and believe they cannot. Jesus, quoting Isaiah to the same effect says, "Hearing you will hear and shall not understand, And seeing you shall see and not perceive; For the hearts of this people have grown dull. Their ears are hard of hearing, And their eyes *they have closed*, Lest they should see with their eyes and hear with their ears, Lest they should understand with their hearts *and turn*, So that I should heal them" (Mt 13:14-15).

Throughout chapters 9–11 Paul purposefully uses the language of appearance to describe phenomena as if it is only

God acting unilaterally, when in reality people are spiritually blind out of their own decisions and choices as well, "And their eyes *they have closed*."[20] We'll see this kind language again with Jacob, Esau and Pharaoh in the next reading.

Their blindness is temporary. Unlike the NFL pre-game talking heads, God foreknows the future with certainty and gives us a glimpse of it in Romans 9–11.

Personal Reflection:

Are there some things concerning God to which you might have "closed your eyes?"

Further Thoughts:

"There are none so blind as those who will not see," says Gary Brandenburg.

I was teaching college kids about the Gospel and emphasizing the point that if anyone seeks Him they will find Him. "He is a rewarder of those who diligently *seek* Him." "*Seek* and you shall find." "You shall *seek* Me and you shall find Me..." In fact God has "pre-appointed our times and boundaries in the hope that we would *seek* Him and touch Him and find Him, and indeed He is not far from each one of us." In other words, He'll surely be found if we seek Him.

Jesus said, "If any man is willing to do His will, he shall know of the teaching, whether I speak from God or on My own." If we seek Him, we'll surely find Him, and we'll find Him in the person of Christ. Zacchaeus casually "sought" to see who Jesus was, and was saved; the book of Acts is replete with God-fearing men and women, seeking God, to whom God brought the Gospel.

One college fellow perceptively raised his hand and asked, "How about the Muslims, they seem so godly, praying seven times a day. They are seeking God... but they're not finding Him in Jesus."

"But *are they* seeking God?" I answered. Look at Matthew 13:15. "For the hearts of this people have grown dull. Their ears are hard of hearing, And their eyes *they have closed*, Lest they should see... *and turn*, so that I should heal them." The fact is so many of the Muslims we see on TV praying in the mosques are not seeking God at all. They are seeking Allah, Mohammed, the Koran and whatever else, but they have *very willfully and dogmatically shut there eyes* to being open about God, or that the Creator might be someone different than Allah. Certainly they are dogmatically closed to the Gospel of Christ. Rather, we can still say strongly, If any man or woman seeks God, they will find Him, and they will find Him in the Person of Jesus Christ (Jn 7:17).

Has God hardened so many of the Muslim's hearts? In the figurative way Paul writes in Romans 9–11, yes. It truly *appears* that way. But that has nothing to do with the fact that the non-believing Muslim would say he is consciously free to do as he pleases in regard to Christ. In their, or our, *choosing* not to see, it could also be said that God has "blinded" us by "giving us over" to our choices that cause us not to see. God's sovereignty includes our freewill—a mystery, but not a contradiction. (See end notes 13 and following).

Group Questions:

1. Have you ever "closed your eyes" to something, become closed-minded? What?
   What causes people to want to close their eyes? In the case of unbelieving Israel, why would so many be content to keep their eyes closed about Christ?

2. The Jews of Paul's day were closed-minded on the issue that God grades on a performance basis ("they...seeking to establish their own righteousness, have not submitted to the righteousness of God"). Why?

3. If you were sharing the Gospel with one who has "closed eyes," what would be your tact?

24

Election

"(for the children not yet being born, nor having done any good or evil,
that the purpose of God according to election might stand,
not of works but of Him who calls),
it was said to her, 'The older will serve the younger.'
As it is written, 'Jacob I have loved, but Esau I have hated.'"
Romans 9:11-13

"For He says to Moses,
'I will have mercy on whomever I will have mercy,
and I will have compassion on whomever I will have compassion.'
So then it is not of him who wills or runs, but of God who shows mercy.
For the Scripture says to the Pharaoh,
'For this very purpose I raised you up,
that I may show My power in you,
and that My name may be declared in all the earth.'
Therefore He has mercy on whom He wills,
and whom He wills He hardens." Romans 9:15-18

"What then? Israel has not obtained what it seeks;
but the elect have obtained it, and the rest were blinded." Roman 11:7

Have you heard of "PEST?" It stands for *Post Election Selection Trauma*, a designation of mental illness by the AHA, American Health Association. AHA president Robert Gordon says it is primarily people who feel "the religious right" is taking their rights away, that the White

House is becoming the "Right" House. PEST "victims" feel that the separation of church and state is being torn down. Gordon recommends as treatment the throwing of darts at a life-size poster of President Bush.

Many people have trauma with the thought of predestination or election being in the Bible. One need not assume that God's election or predestining means fatalism. The Bible clearly teaches freewill *and* sovereignty. God's foreknowledge and election *includes* man's freewill—a mystery, but not a contradiction (Please see "Preface to Romans 9–11" and endnotes 13–21). As mentioned previously, an overly simplistic view of the verses above has been used to support a view of predestination that amounts to fatalism, but actually doesn't square with the rest of the Bible. Let's suggest some things that might clear it up.

First, speaking of election, Peter says we are "elect *according* to foreknowledge" (I Pt 1:20). In Romans 8:29-30, Paul gives the Divine order of salvation, the *ordo saludis*, "whom He foreknew, He also predestined... whom He predestined, these He also called; whom He called, these He also justified; and whom He justified, these He also glorified." Logically, foreknowledge precedes election. That is important since only those who believe are elect. God foreknows who will believe. Therefore they are "elect according to foreknowledge." God's foreknowledge is prior to election logically,[21] but not chronologically, for God's knowledge is instant and eternal. (I'm not saying we can understand this. It is a mystery because our finite minds cannot grasp an Infinite's mind. But we *can* understand it in a way that it is not a contradiction). We should not think of election as

God's capricious, arbitrary, fatalistic act. The Bible affirms His election is *according to foreknowledge* (of freewill acts).

In the case of Jacob and Esau, the fact is God wrestled with Jacob over time and He came to faith. God gave *Esau* all he needed to come to faith also, but he didn't. God did not simply and arbitrarily choose to zap Jacob with salvation and not Esau. His election was according to foreknowledge, not of their works, but of their faith. That He said, "Jacob I loved, but Esau I hated (9:13)," again is the language of appearance. God's actions toward them would have *appeared* as if God "hated" Esau, but God actually loves the *world* (Jn 3:16), *including Esau!* The "hatred," i.e., His actions that were consequences of Esau's choices (e.g., not having faith, being "profane," Heb 11:16-17), was a *holy hatred*, not unlike His wrath and jealousy we have already discussed. As Paul will tell us shortly in 12:9, for love to be without hypocrisy it must "hate" evil.

In the case of Pharaoh one assumes at first reading that God arbitrarily zapped him so that he was hardened. The preceding verses seem to imply God could have had mercy (and made Pharaoh do right), but He didn't. But the Scriptures cannot be understood that way. Namely, in the account of the actual story, God gave Pharaoh miracle after miracle—signs—to do the right thing. Please think about this: God was not hardening Pharaoh; He was giving Him every opportunity to believe and do what He ordered. God was unbelievably *merciful* to Pharaoh!

Pharaoh was already "hardened," God was trying to mercifully *soften* him! Listen to Pharaoh's arrogant, defiant, hardened attitude when Moses first approaches him. "Who is the Lord that I should obey His voice to let Israel go? I do not know the Lord, nor will I let Israel go" (Ex 5:2). He wasn't just defiant, he was incredibly mean-spirited, as seen in the extra quotas and hardness he displayed to the children of Israel as a result of Moses' request (Ex 5:4-21). I probably wouldn't want to give mercy to a guy like that... but guess what? God does. Overflowing mercy.

God multiplied His signs and wonders. During Moses first three miracles the Divine Record says Pharaoh's heart "grew hard," or was "unmoved." At the fourth sign—killing the frogs—Pharaoh "hardened his (own) heart" (Ex 6:15). On the fifth, his heart "grew hard." On the sixth "*Pharaoh* hardened his heart" (8:32), on the seventh his heart "became hard," on the eighth, finally it says, "*the Lord* hardened the heart of Pharaoh" (9:12), followed by *Pharaoh* hardening his own heart again (9:34), then the Lord hardened Pharaoh's heart (10:20), and so on.

Did the Lord harden Pharaoh's heart? Yes.[22] Did Pharaoh have a hard heart beforehand? Yes. Did Pharaoh harden his own heart? Yes. The point? That Pharaoh did as he pleased. God's sovereignty in hardening Pharaoh's heart did not override his freewill at all. It brought out what was already there! Further, the hardening agent was actually God's *mercy!*

What is too often overlooked is that it was God's kindness, His mercy through His many gracious miraculous "signs" that hardened Pharaoh's heart. It wasn't a simple predestined zapping of his heart that hardened it. To put it another way, Pharaoh will never be able to say to God, "*You* made me sin.

You made me do what I did." Rather, God gave him every reason *not to do what he did!* God's mercy in the many miracles and chances was more than reason enough to repent and soften his heart (Rom 2:4).

One might think here of God's kindness and mercy in providing the cross, to the Jews a stumbling stone, but to believers, the power of God unto salvation. "Therefore consider the goodness and severity of God: on those who fell (over the "stumbling block"), severity; but toward you, goodness" (11:22). Why did Jacob believe and Esau not? Why did Pharaoh resist but Moses didn't? Why do some Jews believe and others not? Or so many Gentiles compared to Jews during this period? Why did you believe, but your brother or cousin did not? It is a mystery. *But it is not God's fault that any person disbelieves.* God has given us each all we need to seek Him and come to faith. God's elective purposes might not be as bad as some have thought. If you are suffering from a form of spiritual "PEST," I would suggest *not* to throw darts at Him.

Personal Reflection:

Are there things you blame God for that actually might not be His fault? Things you thought God caused, but He didn't? Have you ever sinned and, subtly or not so subtly, blamed God for it?

Group Questions:

1. How can it be said that God's kindness or His mercy "hardened" Pharaoh's heart?

2. What does "elect according to foreknowledge" mean to you?

3. Which seems harder, election without freewill, or election with freewill and foreknowledge? Why?

25

Confession

(Suggested Reading, Romans 10)

> *"That if you confess with your mouth the Lord Jesus*
> *and believe in your heart that God raised him from the dead,*
> *you will be saved.*
> *For with the heart one believes unto righteousness,*
> *and with the mouth confession is made unto salvation."*
> Romans 10:9-10

Far too many well-meaning people have stumbled over this passage, Romans 10:9-10. I cannot possibly count the times I've been in an evangelistic meeting and heard the speaker destroy an otherwise excellent talk, but more importantly the Gospel of Grace, with the misuse of this verse as an invitation to faith.

Since Romans 10:9 says that one needs to "confess with his mouth the Lord Jesus," or "Jesus as Lord," to be "saved," many have mistakenly assumed such a confession is necessary for justification, or for the reception of eternal life. Nothing could be further from the truth since any "confession" is transparently a "work," and justification, or regeneration, *cannot be of works* (3:24; 4:2-8; Gal 2:16; Eph 2:8-9; Titus 3:4-5, etc.). Some have even mistakenly seen in this passage a basis for a false gospel known as "Lordship salvation," that Jesus must be Lord or Master of one's life to be saved (justified).[2]

While confession of Christ as Lord is not necessary for "salvation" in the sense of justification, it is necessary for the kind of salvation Paul speaks of in Romans. Remember, from early on Paul has made it clear that he is talking about a *salvation* that is "much more" than justification or reconciliation. He's talking about a salvation (or "deliverance") from the present wrath of God through the power of Christ's resurrected life in us (see 1:16-18; 5:9-10, and, "A Much More Salvation," p. 84).

Verse 10 begins to make this clear. Paul gives a brief summary of the book up to this point. "With the heart one believes unto righteousness." This is the imputed righteousness that includes justification and is by faith alone in Christ alone, absolutely apart from works, 3:24–5:10. "(A)nd with the mouth confession is made unto salvation," a summary of the "much more salvation" section of 5:9–8:39.

Lordship salvation proponents, subtle or not so subtle, include public confession of Christ as part of "true faith." They teach that if one is not public about his faith—further, if one does not make Jesus Lord of his life—then he or she has not "really" believed. This is terrible exegesis of what Paul is saying and a lack of sensitivity to the preciseness of his words.

While we agree that the "confession" at hand is a public one, it is something different and subsequent to faith. Three verses later Paul says, "For, 'whoever shall *call upon* the name of the Lord shall be saved'" (10:13). *"Calling upon"* (*epikaleō*) the name of the Lord is a "functional equivalent" to *"confessing"* (*homologeō*) His name as Lord—either results in *salvation*. Both words are used of a public kind of *confession* or *calling-upon* (*epikaleō*—Ac 7:59; 9:14; 22:16; 25:11-12; 2 Tim 2:22; *homologeō*—Mt 7:23; 10:32; Lk 12:8; Jn 1:20; 9:22; 12:42, etc.).

Confessing Christ as Lord, or calling upon Him as Lord, is *different and subsequent* to faith as seen in 10:14-15, "How then shall they *call upon Him* (*epikaleō*) *in whom they have not believed?* And how shall they *believe* in Him of whom they have not heard? And how shall they hear without a preacher? And how shall they preach unless they are sent?" The point is that each item is subsequent and different to the thing that precedes it. To *call upon* the Lord for salvation is understood as *subsequent* to *believing in Him* (for justification), which one cannot do until he hears, and so on.

Calling upon the Lord for Divine aid is what the victorious section of Romans 8 is all about! Appealing to the Sovereign Lordship of our Living Savior is central to experiencing victory over sin and His resurrection life. That is the "salvation" Paul has in mind throughout Romans and, unlike justification, it will require "works" on our part, including "calling upon" and "confessing" Him as Lord.

Now here is the question: Is there such a thing as a "secret believer" who is justified and has eternal life? Certainly. Justification, like the reception of eternal life, is simply a matter of "*belief* in one's heart" before God (Ro 10:10a—Paul is not making any distinction between so-called "heart" faith and "head" faith. He is simply reminding us here of the singular condition for justification [3:24–5:1]. All that is meant by "with the heart one believes…" is that faith is an *inner*, private, personal persuasion. No Biblical study of the word heart will allow the distinction between "head and heart faith" that Lordship proponents make. See reading on "Faith," p. 71ff.).

On the other hand, is there such a thing as a "secret *victorious* believer," experiencing the life and "salvation" Paul envisions in Romans 8? No. Such a victorious life requires calling upon, or "confessing" Christ—open reliance on the life of the resurrected Lord Jesus Christ.

Romans 10:9-10, then, is an effective summary of the book until this point. It, along with its context—especially 10:13-14—affirms our interpretation. Justification is by faith alone "in the heart," apart from works. Salvation in Romans is subsequent to that and *much more*—and also much more than commonly thought.

Personal Reflection:

Have you "believed in your heart"? Would you see yourself as a "secret believer" or an "openly confessing" victorious believer?

Further Thoughts:

I witnessed an evangelistic role-play twenty years ago that makes me shudder to this day. There the jock, a cheerleader, a nerd, a party-animal, a Sunday-school type, etc.—caricatures of real life high school kids. The role-play was ongoing. Over several days you saw the different characters interacting with each other as they studied, planned a party, and hungout. Via personal thought tapes, the audience also got clues as to what was going on inside the characters.

They all end up at an evangelistic camp (like the one where we were). Having heard the speaker they were all pondering what to do with Christ. One of the staff played "Christ," and came and talked with each role player privately. Talking to the football player about the pressure from dad to get the scholarship and other things on the young man's heart, "Jesus" finally tells him, "I want you to give Me your life."

The football jock replied, "Jesus, you know I believed in you when I was eight." The "Christ" role player responded, "Bill, that's not enough. *Until you make Me number one in your life, you're not a Christian.*"

The next day, you can imagine the confused kids who might have thought *believing* was enough based on John 3:16. Now they were unsure. To make matters worse, there was a Questions Seminar that morning. The questions were sad for me to hear, but not nearly as much as the answers the "head counselor" gave. One girl asked, "Do I have to give up anything to be a Christian?" "Yes," the counselor answered, "you'll have to give up friends and…" To be honest, at that point my memory bank runs out—probably because I was so mad that the simple, beautiful gospel of assuring grace had been that badly butchered!

Making Jesus "number One" is great, as is "giving up things" to do so… *but they have absolutely not one thing to do* with receiving the "*free gift* of eternal life." They have everything to do with *discipleship* (see Lk 14:25-33), and maybe something to do with *Lordship*, but not one twit to do with justification, regeneration and reconciliation with God—that's simply by faith alone.

Group Questions:

1. Why is it important, do you think, to be clear on the Gospel?

2. Why, do you think, open confession or calling upon the name of the Lord is necessary for salvation from the present wrath and experiencing the Romans 8 kind of life?

3. How is Romans 10:10 a summary to this point?

26

Presentation

(Suggested Reading, Romans 12)

> *"I beseech you therefore, brethren, by the mercies of God,*
> *that you present your bodies a living sacrifice,*
> *holy, acceptable to God, which is your reasonable service."*
> Romans 12:1

Think back to your favorite Christmas. In particular, think back to your favorite Christmas gift you ever received. What made it such a good gift?

I've had several good Christmases. Two come to mind in particular. When I was twelve I thought my poor baseball skills would be helped if I had a good glove. My parents gave me a Rawlings "Gold Glove." Cost about $25, which was huge in those days—a comparable glove today is $225! I loved that glove for many years—and it did help be a better player (I still wasn't very good, but it made me better than with my bad glove!).

When Austin was just starting, I let him use my old Gold Glove. It gave him a great advantage on the other seven year-olds because compared to their new stiff models, his was so broken-in that it caught the balls for him! (No kidding, the coach got a kick out of it when I asked him to throw me a ball. He was about fifty feet away. He threw it, and I moved out of the way and threw my glove to it. The Gold Glove caught it, came to the ground, and kept the ball inside it even after it landed! That's the kind of glove that is a boy's friend).

In this passage, Paul speaking on behalf of God, says he *beseeches* us, begs us, encourages us, to *present* our bodies a living sacrifice to the Lord. *Present* is a reminder of the same word he used in Romans 6:13ff. where we were told to *present* ourselves and our members as instruments of righteousness to God as those alive from the dead.   Knowing that we're resurrected people, who have the power of Christ's Spirit to make real His resurrection life in our mortal bodies (8:11), Paul is asking us to *present* ourselves as a *living* sacrifice to God. (He's already got enough *dead* ones!)

It was Christmas time my junior year in high school that this verse came alive for me. I had gotten presents for everybody on my list, but I was really serious about giving the Lord a "present." "What could I give Him?" I pondered and prayed. That week it came to me. The best gift I could give Him was my life. I was already a believer, but I knew there was more to life than what I was experiencing. I couldn't put my finger on it, but felt "presenting" my life to Him as a *present* was what He wanted, what had been missing, and what was the best thing I could do.

If you want to give a good present, here are three things to remember. A good present needs to be *considerate, costly*, and *un-coerced*. These are some of the crucial elements for giving good gifts at Christmas and they are crucial in the best gift we can give the Lord, all alluded to here in 12:1.

A good present needs to be *considerate*, thoughtful. Paul says, in light of the *mercies of God* which he has been talking about throughout this book, especially in chapters 9–11, *presenting* our lives to the Lord is only *reasonable* (*logikos*, the word from which we get "logical"). He has done so very much for us in His mercy, especially in the Gift of His Son, it's only *logical* that we would want to give back to Him.

A good present is *costly*. That does not necessarily mean it cost the giver a great deal, though it might, but rather that it is costly in the *receiver's* eyes; it is valuable *to him*, precious to him. Though eternal life is a gift that cost Him to give, giving our lives to Him costs *us*. Beside giving Him our very lives, He wants them to be *holy*—requiring even more cost and effort on our part.

Finally, and perhaps most important to understand, a good present needs to be *un-coerced*. God is not making us give Him this gift. Notice carefully, Paul is talking to *"brethren,"* that is *believers* who are in the family of God. Whether we *present* ourselves to the Lord or not... we're still *brethren!*

Too many times, because of buying into faulty theology, preachers and evangelists choose to tell non-Christians to "commit their lives to Christ" to get eternal life. Where is that in the Bible?! The Bible repeatedly says—over 150 times in the New Testament—the *one thing* a non-Christian needs to do to get eternal life is: *Believe!* Because they have been misled into error themselves, or guilty of their own fuzzy thinking, they have muddied the waters of a clear grace Gospel with works.[2] It does not matter whether they mean well, it's misleading.

God does not *coerce* or force us to commit our lives to Him. The presentation Paul has in mind is a free-gift offering back to God—as free as His was free to us. But remember, if you are a believer, whether you have "committed" your life to Him or not—while it only makes "sense" to do so—you are still a brother or sister in Christ regardless![23]

Personal Reflection:

Have you come to a place in your life where you have committed yourself to Christ?

Further Thoughts:

I was at another evangelistic camp where the speaker had done an excellent job. He had done such a good job of making clear our need for Christ because of our sin. The next night he couldn't have done a better job on the "cross talk," concluding that Christ had "paid it all." But on the "appropriation" talk, he used the Prodigal Son as his text and immediately "left for the far country." (While the Prodigal is a great picture of Christians straying from the Lord, needing to "repent," and come home to the Forgiving Father—it is just that, *for Christians*. After all, the prodigal is a *"son"* for heaven's sake!).

On the night before the speaker had painted a clear picture of Christ dying in our place. But now with the Prodigal he introduced something else. "What do you have to do to receive this gift? *Come home!*" It's as simple as ABC, he went on, "'A'—Admit that you're a sinner. 'B'—Believe that

Christ died for your sins. 'C'—Come home!"[24] (What in the foul ball does *"come home"* mean?! I wondered...)

He concluded, "Christ paid it all, *but it's going to cost you everything.*" Do you think these high school kids were confused? You better believe it! What he might have sloughed-off as "paradox"—*"Christ paid-it-all; it costs-you-everything,"* is not paradox. It's meaningless contradiction!

The fact is, it doesn't cost you *anything* to be a believer and know you are going to heaven. We are "justified *freely* by His grace" (3:24). You don't *give*, you *get!* Whether a believer presents his life to the Lord or not, he is still a *brethren!* Roman 12:1 is a great verse for making this distinction.

Group Questions:

1. Share your favorite Christmas, in particular you favorite gifts received or given.

2. Why does Paul say it is "reasonable," *logical*, that we should present our bodies a living sacrifice?

3. Does one have to "present," or commit, his life to know he is going to heaven?

4. What are some of the advantages, do you think, for giving your life to the Lord?

27

Transformation

"And do not be conformed to this world,
but be transformed by the renewing of your mind,
that you may prove what is that good and acceptable
and perfect will of God."
Roman 12:2

"Try it... you'll like it." As a pre-schooler I remember my mother trying to get me to taste apple juice. It just didn't look right to me. Having two older brothers, you can imagine I was gun-shy at "trying" things. Even my mom might be pulling a fast one. A little guy can't be too careful... I was sure it was vinegar and she was getting ready for a big laugh at my expense. ...But it really was apple juice. I tried it, and of course it was very tasty to a young palate.

I'm known as an amateur connoisseur of good, hole-in-the-wall eating places. When people are going out of town, they'll ask me a spot to eat and generally I can tell them where to go. I get to travel a lot, and when I go to an unfamiliar town, I always ask the locals for the best places. However, I wouldn't know if they were *really* good unless I tried them for myself.

There is no way you are ever going to experience personally how wonderful, how *good and well-pleasing and perfect* God's will is until you: a) Know what it is, and b) try it for yourself.

Paul wants us to be *transformed by the renewing of our minds* so that we can experience how wonderful doing God's will is. To *prove* (*dokimazō*—to approve, test, try, find out) in this case has the idea of finding out and substantiating by personal experience. You won't *taste* how good *God's will* is until you do it; you won't do it until you know what it is; you won't know what it is until you *renew your mind*.

How do we *renew* our minds? The noun (*anakainōsis*) is only used here and Titus 3:5, "according to his mercy He saved us, through the washing of regeneration and *renewing* of the Holy Spirit." The verb is only used two other times, 2 Corinthians 4:16, "Therefore we do not lose heart. Even though the outward man is perishing, yet the inward man is being *renewed* day by day;" and Colossians 3:10, "and have put on the new man who is *renewed* in knowledge according to the image of Him who created him."

Some clues for renewing our minds are these: The renewing is something the *Holy Spirit* does (Titus 3:5). An outside (A)gent is also implied in the other two verses where "being renewed," or "is renewed," are both in the *passive voice*. In other words the *inward man*, or *new man*, is not renewing *himself* (which would require the Greek *middle voice*), but something or someone *outside* of him is doing the renewing. Nevertheless, living according to the Spirit does not mean we are passive (8:1-17). As mentioned, it requires our willpower and having a spiritual mindset (see *Walking According to the Spirit*). Our part in *"renewing"* our minds would include the Spirit-aided obedience of thinking "on the things of the Spirit" which will include attention to the lifestyle commands which follow (the rest of Romans, 12:3ff.), and ultimately all the Scriptures.

The command *"be transformed"* concurs with this. The word *metamorphoō*, the word from which we derive metamorphosis, is only used four times in the New Testament. Twice in reference to the *transfiguration* (Mt 17:2; Mk 9:2), and illustrative of the *transformation* we will experience when we get our glorified bodies.

The only other reference sheds great light on our passage here. The *metamorphosis* of which 2 Corinthians 3:18 speaks is the process of healthy Christian growth, from one stage to the next, which the Holy Spirit produces in us, *transforming* us to the *image* of Christ. We have a vital part in that growth Paul says, "But we all, with unveiled face (he has already explained, that in contrast to the Jew whose heart is still "veiled" in unbelief, the veil is "taken away in Christ" for the believer), *beholding as in a mirror* the glory of the Lord, are being *transformed* into the same *image* from one stage of glory to the next, just as by the Spirit of the Lord" (2 Co 3:18). The miraculous *mirror* in which we see the *image of the glory of the Lord*—Jesus Christ (see 2 Cor 4:4)—and into which we are transformed by the Spirit's transforming work, is none other than the *mirror of God's Word* spoken of in James 1:21-25.

So what is *our part* in the *renewing our minds/transformation* process? It is to pay careful attention to the mirror of God's Word. As we *renew our minds*, reminding ourselves each day in God's Word of who we now are by virtue of the new birth, God's Spirit *conforms* and *transforms* us into Christ. Like the ugly duckling, seeing the beautiful swan and not yet realizing it was himself in the reflection, we too ponder the image of the glory of God—Jesus Christ—in the miraculous mirror of His Word. As you do so, the Spirit causes you to realize,

"This is what you were meant to be." God the Holy Spirit then does His miraculous work, from the inside out, from one glorious stage to the next, of transforming us, "metamorphosizing" us into the image of Christ.

Renewing your mind and speeding-up the transformation process can begin right here. In the practical commands that follow in the rest of Romans (12:3ff.), it will not take a trained eye to see the image of the glory of the Lord—Jesus Christ—from one verse to the next. As you ponder the image, and by the Spirit seek to obey the pattern, see if you don't witness immediate new "family resemblance" to your older Brother. "Try it… you'll like it."

Personal Reflection:

At what stage are you in this Christian transformation? Are you staying in the larvae stage? Caterpillar? Baby butterfly? Full-grown butterfly?—Where are you on the "conformity-to-Christ" growth chart?

Further Thoughts:

My son is reaching young adolescence. He's at a time often characterized by rapid growth spurts. He is fourteen, but just now beginning to get his twelve-year-old molars. Though obviously his growth is accelerating, can you imagine if he got on the scales every day, or measured his height every hour. Even during a rapid growth period, such measurements would be disappointing. Even *rapid* physical growth is by nature relatively slow.

Why would we think spiritual growth is any different? Even if we're doing things basically right, as Paul has outlined in Romans—we're thinking right, presenting ourselves to God, walking by the Spirit, trusting God more, etc.—we could become discouraged that transformation into Christ-likeness is not quite as fast as we thought.

If *experiencing* the life, peace and joy Paul has promised, while hopefully occurring more frequently, is still not as constant as you would like, don't lose heart. The Christian life is a process, a *metamorphosis*, from "one stage of glory to the next." The larvae is not instantly a butterfly.

Group Questions:

1. Renewing our minds has a passive element and an active element. What is meant by that?

2. The Holy Spirit does the renewing and transforming (Titus 3:5; 2 Cor 3:18). What is our part in the process?

3. Can you give an example of how one might see Jesus in the Scriptures, even when He is not mentioned specifically? Would "looking for Jesus" in the Scriptures change your approach to personal Bible study? As you see Him, "the glory of the Lord," what will the Spirit do in your life (2 Cor 3:18)?

28

Application
(Suggested Reading, Romans 12-16)

> *"And do not be conformed to this world,*
> *but be transformed by the renewing of your mind,*
> *that you may prove what is that good and acceptable*
> *and perfect will of God."*
> Roman 12:2

May we extend the *Ugly Duckling* metaphor (which I borrowed from Craig Glickman)? After experiencing such hardships (the Christian growth process will have its own hardships as well, viz. 5:2-5; 8:17-39), the ugly duckling saw his own image in the reflection and realized *he* was the beautiful swan—

> *...no longer a dark, gray bird, ugly and disagreeable to look at,*
> *but a graceful and beautiful swan. —To be born in a duck's nest*
> *is of no consequence to a bird, if it is hatched from a swan's egg.—*
> *He now felt glad to have suffered such sorrow and trouble, because*
> *it enabled him to enjoy so much better all the pleasure and*
> *happiness around him; for the great swans swam around the*
> *newcomer, and stroked his neck with their beaks as a welcome.*

> *(The children came, expressing how beautiful he was. The old*
> *swans bowed their heads before him.) Then he felt quite ashamed,*
> *and hid his head under his wing; for he did not know what to do,*
> *he was so happy, and yet not at all proud. He had been persecuted*

and despised for his ugliness, and now he heard them say he was the most beautiful of all birds. ...Then he rustled his feathers, curved his slender neck, and cried joyfully, from the depths of his heart, "I never dreamt of such happiness as this, while I was an ugly duckling"

When the swan thought he was an ugly duckling, or a cat, or turkey, it is understandable for him to have acted like one. That's what he *thought* he was! It is understandable, too, for believers who think they are still the same old persons they were, addicted and enslaved to sin, to live like the world. We need to constantly be renewing our minds so that we can live in accordance with the "new" person we now are in Christ.

What happened to the "ugly duckling" when he realized, via seeing his true image in the reflection, he was in fact a beautiful swan? First, he wasn't "proud." Neither do we have anything to boast about. We are who we now are by pure grace! (apart from our own works 3:27; 4:2). Second, she started acting like who she was, in accordance with her nature, rustling her feathers, curving her slender neck. No more honking like a goose (hopefully!), or purring like the cat... she was acting like who she was, a beautiful swan.

We now share in Christ's life. His resurrection-brand, overcoming sin, suffering, loving, righteous, joyful, obedient, filled-with-peace kind of life. "If the Spirit of Him who raised Jesus from the dead dwells in you, He who raised Christ from the dead will also give life to your mortal bodies through His Spirit who dwells in you" (8:11). Not just life in heaven, don't you see, but resurrection-powered life right now. Let's live like it! Rustle our feathers and be who we are, whom God, by new life, has made us to be.

That ugly duckling-now-become-beautiful-swan had built-up some bad habits I imagine. She was going to have to learn, not *to be* a swan—she already was one—but to *act* like a swan. There is going to be a learning curve for us, too, to *renew our minds* to thinking and acting like Jesus. When Paul will say shortly, *"Put on the Lord Jesus..."* (13:14), he uses a metaphor of putting Him on like a set of clothes. "Putting on," is also an expression meaning "to act." Unfortunately, it is often used negatively, in reference to people *"putting on* an act" in the sense of being something they are not to gain status or manipulate. When a believer seeks to *act* like Christ, she is not being hypocritical—putting on a front, or play-acting—*she's being who she really is!* We are to *put on Christ!* Start *acting like Christ!*

From here through the rest of Romans Paul shows us through Christian grace-commands exactly what Christ is like, how He would operate and therefore how we are to act and *"put on."* Lord willing, soon it won't be "acting," but through Spirit-enabled habits it will simply come out of our nature. In reality, like the swan, you are not *"acting"* like someone you're not, but simply *being who you are!*

Paul has said in 12:2 that we should not be "conformed to the this world (lit., "age")." To focus on that alone inevitably leads to legalism and arrogant separatism. Our focus should be more on the next part of the verse, the *how-to* of not being conformed to this age. If you'll be *"transformed by the renewing of your mind...,"* believe me you'll be different from the rest!

The remainder of Romans has injunctions like, "Let love be without hypocrisy. Abhor what is evil. Cling to what is good." *That's Christ!* That's how *He* acts. It is a picture of *Him*. If we are *tolerant* of evil, for example, we are actually *conforming to the age*, not to *Christ*. Christ *abhors* evil (and for good reason!). "Renewing our mind" has a primary thought of re-learning, and changing our thoughts to correspond with those of Christ. And in so doing, you won't live anything like the spirit of this present *age*, you'll be living like and experiencing the "Spirit of life in Christ."

"My thoughts are not your thoughts and My ways are not your ways, says the Lord. As the heavens are above the earth, so My ways are above your ways and My thoughts above your thoughts" (Is 55:8-9). We will not have space to treat the remainder of Romans, the "practical" portion as it has been called. *You can do it.* Read his grace-commands and exhortations with this thought in mind: that you want His thoughts to become your thoughts, His ways to become your ways. Ask the Lord, the Spirit, to help you see Christ in those passages. He will help you, and what's more, as *you* work at it *too*, He'll *renew* your *thoughts*, *change* your ways and transform you into Christ's image.

Personal Reflection:

Assuming you are a believer, you have the risen Christ living in you. Are you "acting" like Christ? Or would you say you could do a better job of "putting on" Christ? What do you need to do to improve your ability to "act" like Christ? Why do we have to "work" sometimes at "putting on" Christ?

Further Thoughts:

We looked at how we might "see Christ" in 12:9, let's take another example, the next verse, 12:10a. "Be kindly affectionate to one another in brotherly love." Are you "kindly affectionate with brotherly love" to fellow believers? Recall Christ's affection for the disciples in the Upper Room, calling them *friends*, sharing His heart with them; do you remember the woman healed, trembling with fear, He affectionately comforts, "*Daughter*, be of good cheer…;" or the sinful woman, even at that moment despised by the crowd, "your faith has saved you, go in peace;" even as Judas betrayed Him in the garden, He says affectionately, "*Friend*, what have you done?" *Jesus is "kindly affectionate."* We should be, too.

How can I "put on Christ" in being more kindly affectionate with brotherly love?" Ask the Spirit to help you. Engage your mind. Brainstorm. Visualize. You might think of *church*— going out of your way to be friendlier; your *ministry team*— showing more genuine interests in them, being more caring, asking more questions, letting your guard down a little; your *work*—giving more time to Bob, he's going through a tough time; treat Ed less like an employee and more like a friend; encouraging more… Am I less *affectionate* at *home* than work?…

You get the idea. Look for Christ in the passage. As you ponder on and apply the passage in your situations, with conscious dependence on the Spirit's help to practice it, you'll be acting more and becoming more like Christ and are already becoming more "spiritually minded."

Group Questions:

1. Have you ever felt like an ugly duckling? Can you share a little about it?

2. Looking at the commands in the verses to follow, will you commit, with the Lord's help, to see Christ in them? How do you suspect that will transform you? How does this perspective of looking at these grace-commands differ from how a non-believing Jew might have looked at the commands in the Law?

3. What are some mental processes that go into applying God's Word in your life? What are the most valuable lessons you have received during these 28 readings?

Overview Bible Study for Section I, *Bad News: Judgment*

This section proceeds from Romans 1:1—3:20. Here are some general questions to enhance your reading.

1. Who is the author and what are his three designations (v. 1)? _____

_____

2. Did Paul originate this "gospel" (v. 2)? Who spoke of it prior? _____

3. This Gospel concerns whom (v. 3)? _____

Verses 3 and 4 supply evidence that Christ is both human and divine (Man and God); what is that evidence? _____

_____

4. How would you sum-up verses 8-15 in one or two good sentences? _____

_____

5. In ancient writings they often used "headings" or summary statements as we do. Romans 1:16-17 provides such a summary. Please chew on these two verses a moment. List five or six observations about Paul's theme.

_____

_____

6. A key verse for our understanding of this "gospel" in Romans is 1:18. List two or three things Paul points out about "the wrath." _____

_____

_____

Verses 19-32 are a long continuation of 1:18. What do these verses (19-32) add to your understanding of God's "wrath" in 1:18? _____

_____

_____

7. In 2:1-16 Paul shows that Gentiles without the law (Old Testament Law) are sinners. In 2:16–3:8 he shows that Jews *with* the law are sinners. Powerfully concluding the section, 3:8-20, Paul repeats that "*both* Jews and Greeks (*Greek speakers* = non-Jews, i.e., Gentiles)...are *under sin*... 'There is *none righteous*, no, not one'" (3:9-10). What are some of the ramifications of there being none righteous in 3:19-20?

_____

_____

8. In Romans 3:20, will anyone ever be able to be justified before God by keeping the law? _____.

9. The law can't justify, but it can condemn! In 3:20, what does the law serve to do? _____

Overview Bible Study for Section II
Good News: Justification

The second section of Romans goes from 3:21–4:25. Here are a few questions to help you as you read through this great portion of Scripture. We leave the "bad news" of the last section and begin the "good news," the "gospel" of Romans. The topic is justification and is foundational as Paul builds toward a doctrine of "salvation" (the topic of the next section, Romans 5:9–8:39) that is "much more" than justification—and *justification* is pretty great as we're about to see!

1. Paul now begins in earnest explaining his thematic statement of 1:17, *"For in it the righteousness of God is revealed from faith to faith…"* Now in Romans 3:21-22 Paul says, "But now the *righteousness of God apart from the law is revealed*, being witnessed by the Law and the Prophets, even *the righteousness of God through faith in Jesus Christ*, to all and on all who believe."

    As 1:17 introduces and 3:21-22 begins to elaborate, the "righteousness of God" which is revealed is not a legal righteousness based on the law, but a righteousness based on _____

    Look at Romans 9:30-32 and 10:3-4. The Gentiles "attained" the "righteousness of faith," but much of Israel didn't. Why? _____

2. The "righteousness" based on the law, is not a "righteousness" that justifies one before God. What does Romans 3:20 and 28 say in that regard? _____
_____

Paul says about this, "I do not nullify the grace of God for if righteousness comes through the law then Christ died needlessly" (Gal 2:21). In light of this, fill in the blank, "If one can be made right with God through the law then
_____

In Philippians 3:9 Paul says he is not counting on "his own righteousness from the law" but the "righteousness
_____

3. In Romans 3:24 list three aspects of justification: _____
_____

4. We are justified through Christ's *redemption*. What is that? _____. What is "propitiation" (v. 25)?_____
_____
Look-up I John 2:2. Christ is said to be the "propitiation" not only for our sins but _____

5. In Romans 3:28 Paul says "we conclude that a man is justified by _____ apart from _____

6. Sum up Romans 4:1-8 in one or two sentences. _____
_____

An Overview Study for Section III
More Good News: Victory!

Romans 5:1–8:39 contains the climax of the book, the full-elaboration of how to be saved from God's present wrath (Romans 1:16-18). The Christian life experience is intended by God to be "much more" than the static doctrine of justification and even the peace, or reconciliation that results. It is a life of peace to be sure, but it is also a dynamic life of dependence, victory, hope (with an eternal perspective), and experiential awareness of God's great love—even through suffering and troubles.

1. In Romans 5:1 justification is in a "past perfect" tense. According to this verse, a summary of 3:24–4:25, what does one need to do to be justified? _____. What is the result? _____

   The "peace" we have with God is experiential through faith, but it also speaks of our reconciled standing with God (see 5:10). What does reconciliation mean to you?

   _____

2. We are not just in a static state of "peace" with God. The next verse, 5:2, says we have access to something else by faith. What is it? _____

3. Romans 5:3-5 gives a preview of some of the topics to be covered. Make note of the words *hope, glory, tribulations (troubles), perseverance, proven character* and the *love of God* "poured out in our hearts by the *Holy Spirit*." Now read Romans 8:16-39. Note these themes and words again. Jot

down where you see them repeated and how Paul
elaborates them. _____

_____
_____
_____

4. How is God's love, poured out in our hearts,
   demonstrated in the death Christ died for us? In other
   words, explain Romans 5:6-8. _____

_____

5. In Romans 5:9-10, what are we "saved" from and list
   some of the ways this "salvation" is different than the
   justification/reconciliation to which it is contrasted.

_____
_____
_____

6. In 5:17, "much more those who receive abundance of
   grace and of the gift of righteousness will *reign in life*..."
   What does reign in life connote to you? _____

_____

7. In Romans 6:1-10, that we are dead and now alive is based
   on what? _____
   What are the resulting commands of Romans 6:11-13?

_____

8. We have been set free from sin (6:18, 22). But when we
   were slaves of sin (or when we've allowed ourselves to be
   to be "re-captivated," see Romans 7:22), what "fruit" did
   we have from those things (6:21)?

9. We have also died to the law. Now we can be "married" to Him who was raised from the dead. What sort of "fruit" should that union produce? (see 6:22 for an example) _____

10. In Romans 7:13-25 Paul shares his struggle as he walked according to the flesh rather than the Spirit. Walking according to the flesh could be something as "harmless" as trying to please God through my own self-efforts and willpower alone. How does Paul describe that experience?

   _____

11. Too many Christians leave their lives in Romans 7 and don't go on to Romans 8! In Romans 8:1-13, list what Paul says are the keys for living victoriously over the law of sin and death _____

   _____

12. The answer to Paul's question, *"Who will deliver me from this body of death?"* is in Romans 8:11. How will the Lord give "life" to our "mortal" bodies? _____

13. Based on Romans 8:13, what is the result of living "according to the flesh"? _____. How does Paul's experience, described in 7:13-25, reflect that kind of death? _____
   "But if by the Spirit you put to death the deeds of the body, you will live." In what regards do you think he means, "you will live?" _____

14. What is the theme in Romans 8:17-39? _____

Overview Study for Section IV
Good News: Summary

Section IV extends to the end of the book, chapters 9–16. We will only discuss up to the beginning of chapter 12 due to time. Chapters 9–11 deal with God's salvation program for Israel and the Gentiles during this age. Chapters 12–16 deal with instructions for individuals, churches in general, and later the Roman believers in particular.

1. In Romans 9:2, why does Paul say he has sorrow and continual grief in his heart? _____

2. In God's elective purpose ("the purpose of God according to election," 9:11), His predestining, at first glance, might seem unfair. Yet we know that God is just and fair, "Shall not the Judge of all the earth do right?" (Gen 18:25); "Is it not my ways which are fair, and your ways which are not fair?. . ." (see Ezekiel 18:25, 29). Can you make sense of Romans 9:12-18 in a way where God is fair? _____

3. Romans 9:19 closes with the question, "For who has resisted His will?" Can you think of someone who has "resisted" His will? _____

4. Romans 9:20-21 reads as if we didn't have any freewill. Can you cite any Scripture to the effect that in fact we do have freewill? _____

5. In 9:30 we read that the Gentiles, not pursuing righteousness, nevertheless attained "the righteousness of faith." Look at 9:31-31. Why did many in Israel not attain that same righteousness? _____

6. As we have argued throughout this book, that "salvation" in Romans is much more than justification, do you see Romans 10:9-10 in a different light than you may have before? That is, do you believe public confession of Christ is necessary to be saved from hell? Why or why not? _____
_____

   Romans 10:14 says confession is something different and subsequent to simple faith. How do you know that based on this verse? _____

7. Read Romans 11:6 with a King James or New King James Bible. It is in the form on an incontrovertible syllogism. In cannot be misinterpreted. What does it say? _____

8. In 12:1 Paul uses the word "present" again (see 6:13). He gives two lines of reasoning why we should present our bodies to the Lord. What are they? _____
_____

9. In 12:2, the way not to be "conformed" to this world is to be _____
   Once you do this, what will you discover about God's will? _____

NOTES

1. The hypothetical argument in 3:5 is, "But if our unrighteousness demonstrates the righteousness of God, what shall we say? God is unjust who inflicts wrath?" In other words, how could God be "just" to inflict wrath on me if my unrighteousness works itself out for the "good" of showing how righteous God is?

In 3:7 he adds, "For if the truth of God has increased through my lie to His glory, why am I also still judged a sinner?" In either argument, the interlocutor is not debating his sin, which he calls "unrighteousness" in v. 5 and "lie" in v. 7, but is trying to reason to the effect that God is not just to inflict wrath. Though he all but admits a sin by referring to his "lie," he hopes to prove that he's really not sinful, "Why am I still judged a sinner?"

Behind both arguments is an implicit bitterness at God, seen in the twisted logic that God's righteousness and glory is either: 1) the result of the person's sin, or 2) the reason his sin is not really sin. Similar to a perverted view of God's sovereignty which would have God be the author of sin rather than freewill creatures.

2. Some theologians feel compelled to add adjectives to simple faith which the Bible does not, like "true faith," "saving faith," "real faith," etc. They feel compelled to do this because of imposing their theology on the text, rather than letting the text say what it says. The Bible does not add adjectives or qualifiers to the word faith in the 150 times it is used to tell us that "belief" or "faith" is the only condition we need meet for the reception of eternal life (it is the same word in the original, the verb *pisteuō* and the noun *pistis*). The Greek word for faith means just that, *faith*. It is the same faith one uses in everyday life. The same faith you have for believing China exists, or the everyday faith of believing what someone tells you is the truth, is the exact same kind of faith by which one receives justification and eternal life. It is a matter of believing Christ at His word that all I need to do is believe Him for eternal life (Jn 1:12; 3:16; 5:24; 6:47, et al).

Salvation, Paul says, is by grace, through faith, *apart from works*, "For by grace you have been saved through faith, and that not of yourselves; it is the gift of God, *not of works* lest any man should boast" (Eph 2:8-9). Faith is not a work; it is in accordance with grace (Ro 4:16). Nor is it a "gift" per se—we all have the ability to believe. The Greek form (in Eph 2:8-9) does not allow the *"that"* to refer to *faith* (*touto* is neuter and *tēs pisteōs* is feminine), the *"that* (which is) not of yourselves" refers to the whole salvation-by-grace-through-faith gift of God (*to dōron*, "the gift" is also neuter).

Because of a misinterpretation of James 2:14-26, some interpreters have assumed that "true, saving" faith inevitably has to produce works, or it was not "saving" faith to begin with. Trying to synthesize the two— Paul's claim for "justification by faith apart from works," and James "justification by faith and works" (or, adjusted by the interpreters to make it fit their theology, "justification by a faith *that produces works*")—the clear waters of a grace-apart-from-works gospel have been muddied.

Interpreted as they commonly are, they contradict one another. The Calvinistic synthesis does not help. Trying to avoid a salvation by works, or the Catholic doctrine of salvation by faith *and* works, the Calvinist will say it is a salvation by "a faith that works (i.e., produces works)." The clever wording does not help a thing. Putting works on the back-end rather than the front, like the Catholics they oppose, does not avoid a works salvation. *Either view is a de facto salvation by works, period.* Over and over Paul says it is "apart from works" (lest we should boast). The Calvinist might rejoin, "But it is not *us* doing the works, but God through us, by faith." Nevertheless, *it necessitates works*, and again, Paul says it is *apart from works*, period.

The disagreement is important for a number of reasons, namely that the Bible is clear that one's assurance of salvation is at the moment of faith, apart from works (Jn 6:47; Ro 5:1; I Jn 5:13, etc.) If faith necessarily has to produce works to be "saving faith" as some theologians claim, immediate, objective assurance is impossible, for one cannot know until heaven, logically, if he or she had faith that persevered in enough good works to qualify as "saving faith"! —Such teaching actually turns the beautiful gospel of grace on its head. As a doctoral candidate in psychology at USC once said, having been under this Calvinistic form of teaching, "I felt like God had me dangling over hell by a string. The string was unraveling... and God didn't give a damn." Unfortunately this is the logical outcome of such a doctrine to those who are serious and sensitive thinkers.

The fact is, even as believers, we still sin—even the most committed of us. John, James and Paul include themselves in saying that we all (including themselves!) continue to stumble in many ways, and that even at our best point of fellowship with Christ, we would be naïve to think we don't have at least some sin (even if unknown to us, see Jas 3:2; I Jn 1:8). How much sin can we do, or for how long—according to the Calvinistic or Catholic paradigms—before we would know that we aren't saved? Obviously, such an important question—if their views were valid—goes unanswered by either, and if attempts are made to answer, they are so obviously arbitrary as to be silly. The Bible would have dealt with this question if it were an issue. How much we sin, or for how long, frankly is not an issue at all in the Gospel of grace, or in the Bible which teaches it.

Then how about James 2:14-26? For the present space, only a few things need to be said. First, James in no way contradicts Paul or John, that faith alone in Christ alone gives eternal life. If this is James, the leader of the Jerusalem church, at the Jerusalem council in Acts 15 he gave his seal of approval on the gospel that Peter and Paul were preaching to the Gentiles, by faith apart from works.

Secondly, there are obviously two kinds of justification: one before men, and one before God. Paul is talking about justification *before God*: "by the deeds of the law shall no flesh be justified *in His sight (enōpion*—before someone, in his presence, in his sight);" "If Abraham was justified by works (a third class condition that implies there *is* a justification by works!) he has something to boast about, but not *before God (pros*—in front, before; "But that no one is justified by the law in the *sight of God* is evident, *para tō theō*). James is talking about outward justification *before men*, which can only be known by "works" of some sort. He says as much. "Do *you* see," James says, speaking of how Abraham proves a justification "by works" (James words) before men when he offered Isaac (Jas 2:21-22). "*You* see," James repeats, going on about something *we can*

169

see, not just God, "that a·man (better, simply "man") is justified by works and not only of faith." To read it as "and not by faith *only*" or "by faith *alone*" as most translations unfortunately do—implying a justification by faith *and* works—is incorrect since "only" (*monon*) modifies the verb *justified*, not the noun *faith* (which would demand the feminine *monēs*)! If one keeps this distinction in mind, that there indeed are two kinds of justification—one before men and one before God, and that the only justification for eternal life is *before God* (Paul's subject)—then we are more than half-way home.

Thirdly, when James asks, "Can faith save him?" The Greek expects a "no" answer. Some translations say, "Can *that* faith save him?," i.e., the faith without works he has just mentioned (Jas 2:14). It is very inconsistent to translate the article in such a way. The more objective King James scholars, and most bonafide scholars today, would say that it should be simply, "Can faith save him?" "No," it can't. Not how James is using the word "saved."

We shouldn't assume that every time a New Testament writer uses the word "save(d)" that he is referring to eternal salvation. That is known as the totality transfer fallacy. (The fact is, the Bible is more likely to use the words *sōzō* or *sōtēria* [save, salvation] to refer to a *temporal* deliverance of some kind: In Philippians Paul says their prayers will turn out for his "deliverance" [1:19]; the woman with the issue of blood was "healed" [*sōzō*]; the saving of a life, Lk 6:9; Mt 8:25; "rescuing" a drowning man, Mt 14:30, and so forth.

When we use the word in English, the context likewise determines the meaning. "*Saved* by the bell," might mean I avoided a tough question as the bell rung; "*Safe* at home," I slid ahead of the tag, got to home plate, or simply am in the secure confines of my house. "Did you *save* that document" brings to mind the preservation device on a computer. ...If the doctor came to the waiting room to report on the near-fatal ruptured appendix of grandad, and the just performed appendectomy proclaiming, "We *saved* him!" do you think that means he shared the gospel with him and grandad accepted? Probably not... Context determines meaning and we shouldn't assume James automatically is talking about "salvation from hell" just because he uses the word *save*...)

This first century audience James is addressing didn't take "save" as referring automatically in the *sometimes* Pauline sense of the word, referring to eternal salvation. "Saved" from what? James has already used the word and will again, both with temporal meanings. In 1:21, James begins this section (ending in 2:26) about being a *doer of the Word.* "Therefore, laying aside all filthiness and overflow of wickedness, in humility receive the implanted word which is able to save your souls." He calls them "brethren" throughout the epistle (1:2, 19; 2:1, etc.), and said that they had been "brought forth (born) by the Word of truth" (1:18). Make no mistake, James considers his audience "regenerate." So when they are to "receive the implanted word (literally, "innate" word, part of their nature via the new birth brought about by this same Word, 1:18) *which is able to save your souls*" he is not saying they might need sometime to get saved again! Rather he is saying that this innate word is able to save one's life from the *premature physical death* that results from not being a doer of the Word! He has just alluded to this as well—the phenomena that all sin, left unchecked, leads to physical death—"when lust is conceived it gives birth to sin, and sin, when it is full-grown, brings forth death," 1:15. ...To "save one's soul" is a well-attested Greek idiom that simply meant "to save one's life" and ought not have the theological baggage with which we might want to invest it.

Finally, at the end of the epistle, James says, "My *brethren*, if any among *you* strays from the truth, and one turns him back, let him know that he who turns a sinner from the error of his way will save his soul from death, and will cover a multitude of sins" (5:19-20). First, he is expressly talking to believers. Second, unless one believes he can lose his eternal salvation (which contradicts every gospel passage, Jn 3:16, 5:24; 6:47, et al), James is transparently talking about "saving the life" of a believer who has gotten away from being a doer of the Word. *Saving* his physical life!

Now back to James 2:14, "can faith save him?" that is, a faith without works? No! Faith without works will not save one's life from the physical consequences of sin, namely the death which comes from failing to be a doer of the Word. James is simply being proverbs-like practical. "If I'm a believer," he might say, "and a jealous husband stands over me with a shotgun for committing adultery with his wife, 'faith alone' is not going to save me!" Had I been a doer of the word, as James is concerned with in this section (1:21–2:26), I wouldn't be in that predicament! Indeed the "implanted word is able to save my life!" (1:21).

Finally, Calvinstic or Catholic students alike will say that faith—"head" faith or "intellectual" assent, as they pejoratively put it—is "not enough." The "demons believe and tremble," James says (2:19). Three quick responses. First, demons aren't savable. Second, the Greek text demands that a hypothetical arguer is speaking, not James (The Greek text does not use quotation marks, but the common way of knowing when the interlocutor stops and the writer begins again is with the expression, "But," and especially when coupled with "O man," or "O foolish man." The arguer of 2:18 is speaking until 2:20. Most translations begin the quotes too soon. For some reason, translators don't miss it in other parts of the NT! See, I Cor 15:35-36, where Paul employs the same technique).

Thirdly, the "formula" that the demons are believing is not "saving" anyway! The hypothetical arguer is saying, "James, you believe that *God is one*, and you do well; the demons believe and tremble." Belief in one God, *monotheism*, saves no one. Every orthodox Jew in James day was a monotheist, as is every Muslim today. Rather, the arguer is trying to show that faith and works are not related, but James says they are.

Works are a major element in maturing our faith, as it did Abraham's, helping us become a "friend of God," as he was, justified before men. Further, works are what keep our faith from becoming cold and dead. In fact this point is missed in every commentary I know of (except the one I most highly recommend, *The Epistle of James*, by Zane C. Hodges). The last verse, 2:26, states, "As the body without the spirit is dead, so faith without works is dead also." Works are the animating spirit that makes faith alive, not vice versa! Yet the commentary literature says quite the reverse, unremittingly assuming their point that *faith must produce works*. This is not James point at all. If one came upon a dead body, obviously it was alive at one time! James is not questioning the reality of whether his readers have faith and eternal life, rather he is exhorting them to have works with their faith lest it become cold, dead and sterile.

We should want to have works with our faith, but if we buy into the idea works are necessary for knowing we have eternal life, not only have we succumbed to a "false gospel," ruled out objective assurance, made nonsense of the most beautiful words ever spoken, "Most assuredly I say to you, whoever believes in Me has everlasting life," but we have put the yoke back on ourselves and others "which neither we nor our forefathers were able to bear."

In a debate over this "saving nature" of faith, a leading radio Lordship teacher used James 2:14-26 to prove that "saving faith will inevitably produce works, or it is not saving faith." His conclusion being that "true" faith is akin to *commitment, surrender* and the like. Dr. Radmacher presented the opposing paper. First, one cannot take a word, *pistis*, well-founded to the nth degree in the annals of lexicography, and make it mean anything one wishes. The word has a long, established and limited meaning—faith, belief, trust. Those definitions fit perfectly in every New Testament text. In fact, very often used in contrast to the first speaker's intention (i.e., *"by faith apart from works"*). Second, the hundreds of clear Biblical usages of it determine its meaning, too. "To take an obscure and debatable passage like James 2:14-26 and let it be the tail that wags the dog is unsound. Rather, the hundreds of clear passages should wag the tail. James 2:14-26 should be re-examined, not the others." Dr. Radmacher went on to suggest Zane Hodges' interpretation of James 2:14-26 as a place to start.

3. There are too many substitution passages to list… Here are just some which employ *hypēr*:

"The Good Shepherd gives his life *for* the sheep… I lay down My life *for* the sheep" (Jn 10:11, 15);
"it is expedient that one man die *for* the people, and not that the whole nation should perish…(prophesying that Jesus would die for the nation)" (Jn 11:50-51);
"Greater love has no man than this, than to lay down one's life *for* his friends" (Jn 15:13);
"He who did not spare His own Son but freely gave Him up *for us* all, how will He not also with Him freely give us all things?" (Rom 8:32);
"Do not destroy with your food the one for whom Christ died" (Rom 14:15)

"This is My body which is broken *for* you." (I Cor 11:24);

"Christ died *for* our sins according to the Scriptures" (I Cor 15:3);

"If One died for all, then all died; and he died for all, that those who live should live no longer for themselves..." (2 Cor 5:14-15);

"For He made Him who knew no sin to be sin *for* us, that we might become the righteousness of God in Him" (2 Cor 5:21);

"I live by faith in the Son of God who loved me and delivered Himself up *for* me" (Gal 2:20);

"Christ has redeemed us from the curse of the law having become a curse *for* us" (Gal 3:13).

"And walk in love, as Christ also has loved us and given Himself *for* us" (Eph 5:2);

"As Christ loved the church and gave Himself *for* her" (Eph 5:25);

"(our Lord Jesus Christ) who died *for* us" (I Thes 5:10);

"Who gave Himself a ransom *for* all" (I Tim 2:6);

"Who gave Himself *for* us, that He might redeem us" (Titus 2:14);

"Christ suffered *for* us" (I Pt 2:21);

"For Christ also suffered once *for* sins, the Just of the unjust, that He might bring us to God" (I Pt 3:18);

4. It is *apropros* for Paul to use the concept of reconciliation in 5:10. "For if while we were enemies we were *reconciled* through the death of His Son...," then in 5:11, "we exult in God through our Lord Jesus Christ through whom we have received the *reconciliation*." The very word connotes a new beginning and that's where we are as Paul turns the corner to talk about the ABC's of starting out on the Christian life.

One thinks of a married couple whose marriage was in trouble, but after counseling or "working it out" through personal negotiations, they become "reconciled." The barriers are broken down to start anew. In fact, one of Paul's first points in this section is that we, too, have been *raised* to walk in *newness of life*. Do we get back under the law? Do we continue in sin? No, that is his purpose in the section—to show how this new reconciled relationship is to continue healthy, filled with joy and peace and hope. The means for the intimate, close relationship God wants for us is laid out in 5:9–8:39. While we will continue to be reconciled forever with the Lord through the death of His Son, there are things we need to believe and do in our new relationship with Him to cultivate it and have a deep, intimate friendship. There is more to the Christian life than just believing Christ for justification... "You are My *friends* if you do whatever I command you" (Jn 15:14). Let's see how to go deeper in our relationship with Christ in Romans 5–8, paying especially close attention to his conclusions in ch. 8...

5. I am much indebted to my professor, mentor and friend, Zane Hodges, for pointing this out to me years ago—the 5:9-10 hinge and the "much more salvation" pointing back to the present wrath of 1:18.

6. The understanding that the "salvation" in the book of Romans is more than justification and includes the deliverance from God's temporal wrath (1:18) also clears up a much misunderstood passage later in the book, Romans 10:9-10. Often used as an appropriation verse in evangelistic presentations, many have assumed that confessing Christ as Lord, or submission to His Lordship, is necessary for the reception of the gift of eternal life. "If you confess with your mouth the Lord Jesus and believe in your heart that God raised Him from the dead, you will be saved. For with the heart one believes unto righteousness, and with the mouth confession is made unto salvation."

The salvation he speaks of though, in Romans, is more than the "salvation" of receiving eternal life. This is evident in 5:9-10, but also in the verses to follow, 10:13-14. Namely, "whoever calls on the name of the Lord shall be saved" (10:13) "Calling upon" His name is a functional equivalent to "confessing" His name and evidently refers to a "public" confession or "calling upon," as the word (*epikaleō*) and confession (*homologeō*) commonly denote in the New Testament (*epikaleō*—Ac 7:59; 9:14; 22:16; 25:11-12; 2 Tim 2:22; *homologeō*—Mt 7:23; 10:32; Lk 12:8; Jn 1:20; 9:22; 12:42, passim).

So, in Romans 10:14, When Paul says, "How shall they call upon Him (*epikaleō*) in whom they have not believed? How shall they believe in Him whom they have not heard? How shall they hear without a preacher..." It is obvious that "calling upon" Him is subsequent and *much more* than just believing, as the progression is to show you cannot have what follows before having what precedes it.

With that understanding, Romans 10:9-10 makes perfect sense without contradicting the free grace message of justification by faith alone. Namely, verse 10 is a summation of the justification followed by Christian life sections of the book. "For with the heart one believes resulting in righteousness (Rom 3:31-5:8), and with the mouth confession is made resulting in salvation (from present wrath, 5:9ff.). Prompting Zane Hodges to note, "Is there such a thing, then, as a secret believer who is justified?" Yes, because faith is in the heart and justification is "before God." "Is there such a thing, then, as a secret, victorious believer?" No, because the dynamic, victorious life spoken of in 5:9ff. requires our "calling upon" the Lord in dependence for help to keep His commands, some of which necessarily imply public confession Lord Jesus Christ (e.g., service in the Christian church).

7. The word translated "tutor" is *paidagōgos*, the word we get pedagogy— the science of teaching. It is from two words, *paidion*—child, and *agō*—to lead. In classical usage a *paidagōgos* was the tutor or "slave who went with a boy from home to school and back again" (Liddel and Scott). The Law does that for us. In effect it takes us by the hand and leads us to Christ by showing us our sins, and that it cannot justify (Ro 3:20; Gal 3:21-25). Its sacrifices are incomplete, offered year after year, unable to actually take away sins, but simply foreshadowing and pointing to the once-and-for-all sacrifice of Christ (contrast Heb 10:3-4 with 10:10, 14).

8. In a few verses he will expound, in *"newness* of the Spirit, not in oldness of the letter" (7:6). The new life in grace, lived with the helping enablement of God's Holy Spirit, as opposed to the old Jewish—and modern legalistic Christian—way of understanding living under the law. The law which was powerless to help us keep it, "weak as it was through the flesh," (8:3).

9. A *caviat* should be said here. When we say you "don't have to sin any more," we are talking about known sin, sin that you are aware of or have a conscience about. We are not at all talking about "sinless perfection," a

176

state that will only be arrived at in heaven (I Jn 3:2). James, Jesus brother, includes himself when he says matter-of-factly, "For we all stumble in many ways." (Jas 3:2). John says that even at our best moment of fellowship, walking in the light, and therefore being aware of no known sin, we have sin and are naïve to think we don't, "If we (including himself!) say we have no sin, we deceive ourselves, and the truth is not in us." Paul's point in Romans is that we don't have to be beset by sin—or any addiction. Through His Spirit we can live victoriously over it (Rom 8:1-14).

10. The standard old Greek lexicon of NT words, "BAG"—Baur, Arndt Gingrich—specifically says about *katakrima*, the word often translated "condemnation" in Roman 8:1, "*Katakrima* is probably not 'condemnation,' but the punishment following sentence, punishment, doom," (Wm. F. Arndt, F. W. Gingrich, *A Greek-English Lexicon of the New Testament and Other Early Christian Literature*. [Chicago: The University of Chicago Press, 1957], p. 413).

11. Setting our minds on the things of the Spirit certainly would include His Word. As Christ is the Agent of the Trinity in creating the world (Jn 1:3; Col 1:16), the Holy Spirit is the Trinitarian Agent who created the Word (2 Pt 1:12; 2 Tim 3:16-17).

12. "For what the law could not do weak as it was through the flesh, God did: sending His own Son in the likeness of sinful flesh and as an offering for sin, He condemned sin in the flesh" (Rom 8:3). The law was *weak* in that it gave us no power or pattern to keep its demands. God not only gives us the Divine *power* through the Spirit (Rom 8:13), but through His Son, He gives a flesh and blood *pattern* to follow (8:3). Christ has condemned, *katakrinō*, pronounced judgment, on sin in the flesh; *we* carry out that penalty phase on sin when "*by the Spirit* we *put to death* the deeds of the body" (8:13).

13. For more on the subject of the compatability of human freedom and Divine foreknowledge, we recommend William Lane Craig's, *The Only Wise God: The Compatability of Divine Foreknowledge and Human Freedom* [Grand Rapids: Baker Book House, 1987]. Calvinists and others will often argue philosophically against freewill by saying that if God

foreknows all future events, then they must be determined. Craig meets this head-on in the preface, "*"Qué será, será*...what will be will be'...is true, but (to say) 'what will be must be' is an expression of fatalism." He then goes on to prove in the book that just because God knows everything in advance does not mean that it is forced and not free.

God's foreknowledge is not a cause of what we do any more than my "knowledge" of what freewill creatures will do causes them to do so. Let's say I know Marci is going to have her devotions at 6:30 am tomorrow. There's good reason for "knowing it," she has done so for twenty years straight, let's say. Granted my knowledge is not perfect like God's—I could be mistaken, she could get sick, the rapture could take place, etc. But nevertheless my "knowledge" of what she will (probably) do has nothing to do with her doing it! Why would we assume God's foreknowledge is otherwise. It isn't.

Craig holds to a positon known as middle-knowledge, or Molinism, after a Jesuit priest named Luis de Molina who came up with his position in the 1600's to answer the determinism of the Reformers. Middle knowledge says that God not only knows all the decisions and acts of freewill creatures, He also knows all the things they would have done if under different times, constraints or stimuli. As well, He knows all the permutations and outcomes of those potential choices as well. Being all wise He knows how to persuade us to do what He wants; being all loving He will do so, but since we have true freewill, there is no guarantee that we will do as He wants.

This is seen for instance in Acts 17:26-27. God has determined and "pre-appointed" our times and boundaries in the hope that we would seek Him and touch Him and find Him, "and indeed He is not far from each one of us". . . *but there is no guarantee we will do so*. The Bible says God "desires (wills) that all be saved and come to a knowledge of the truth," *but we know not all will be*. In other words, in love He is not going to override our freewill. There are things He sincerely wants which, because of our freedom, are not going to happen. "It's not God's will that any perish, but that all come to repentance" (2 Pt 3:9). Moving C.S. Lewis to say God is not a "Divine rapist," He doesn't force us to love Him. "He woos, but He never ravishes." Christ "wills" to gather us as a hen gathers her chicks, but too often we are "unwilling." There are two kinds of people ultimately, as Lewis says, "Those who say, 'Thy will be done,' and those to whom God will say, in the end, '*Thy* will be done'" (*The Great Divorce*, p. 72).

In extreme reaction to hard-Calvinism, a new theology has begun called "open theism." Open theists teach that because we have true freewill, the future is "open," and that even God can't know that part of the future (otherwise it would be forced). Their whole premise against Divine foreknowledge of free acts fails, as the Calvinist's fails against freewill, for the same reason as Craig showed above. Foreknowledge is not a cause of freewill acts; they are compatible. Arguing against one of the leading opennists, Gregory Boyd, Craig comments,

> Boyd's problem is that the only alternatives he knows
> are either Calvinistic determinism or openness. His essay
> shows no awareness of the Molinist alternative.
> Luis de Molina developed his view precisely in response to
> the theological determinism of Calvin and Luther, and the
> *brilliance of his achievement is that he did so without sacrificing
> divine sovereignty.* Unfortunately, contemporary
> open theology sprang up as a reaction to Calvinism in ignorance
> of the Molinist alternative. Are openness theologians so
> entrenched in their perspective that, now having learned
> Molinism, they will persist in their overreaction to Calvinism?
> Or are they willing to accept the more moderate *rapprochement*
> afforded by Molina? (*Divine Foreknowledge, Four Views*.
> Edited by James K. Beilby and Paul R. Eddy [Downers Grove,
> Ill.: InterVarsity Press, 2001], p. 59, italics added).

Often times people are attracted to Calvinism because of the "security" it provides. Please know there is a better and more Biblical alternative (in my view), that neither gives up the security of the believer (Whoever believes "has *eternal life*" Eternal life can't be taken away, or Christ should have called it something else!) nor the freewill of man. Nor does it go to the other heretical extreme of openness, denying God's omniscience and sovereignty. Ultimately the question is, which perspective fits the Bible best.

14. In real life, George MacDonald had been a famous Scottish Christian author in the 1800's. Though he died around the turn of the century (1824-1905), his books had a tremendous influence on Lewis as a young man. In his autobiography, *Surprised By Joy*, Lewis credits MacDonald's *Phantastes* with beginning the process of his conversion from skepticism to Christianity. He considered MacDonald his mentor, "I have never concealed the fact that I regarded him as my master; indeed I fancy I have never written a book in which I did not quote from him" (*George MacDonald: An Anthology*, ed. by C.S. Lewis, 1946, p. 20).

15. C.S. Lewis, *The Great Divorce* [MacMillan: New York, 1946], p. 72. This confession about hell comes from the lips of a former universalist. When Lewis discovers the guide is George MacDonald he says, "What are *you* doing here? I thought you were a universalist." MacDonald, in his writings, seemed not to believe in hell, or that it was only temporary. "I was, but I was wrong," comes the reply.

16. Scientific naturalism is a philosophical outlook dedicated to exalting empirical science while dogmatically holding to only natural explanations, denying as legitimate any metaphysical or Divine causes. Scientific naturalism leads to a philosophy called *reductionism*. Reductionism reduces us to chemicals. Most scientific naturalists and all reductionists are "biological determinists." Naturalist William Provine admits, *"Free will as it is traditionally conceived... simply does not exist... There is no way that the evolutionary process as it is currently conceived can produce a being that is truly free to make choices."* Physicist John Searle concurs, *"our (naturalistic philosophy's) conception of physical reality simply does not allow for radical freedom (viz. freewill)."* (J.P. Moreland and Scott B. Rae, *Body & Soul, Human Nature & the Crisis in Ethics* [Downers Grove, Illinois: InterVarsity Press, 2000], p. 240). Searle, as so many scientists, has turned from physics to philosophy.

Such thinking (reductionism) presumes the acceptance of naturalistic philosophy. With the dogmatism of not allowing the possibility of other views, *scientific naturalism (and reductionism) is a religion*—an anti-supernatural religion. Molecules and chemistry being what they are determine what the things do, they say. This is called *biological determinism*. Searle, trying to deny the existence of a soul as the explanation for mental processes, pontificates, (for freewill to be true), "...we would have to postulate, that inside each of us [our physical bodies] was a self that was capable of interfering with the causal order of nature… we would have to contain some entity that was capable of making molecules swerve from their paths" (*Body and Soul*, 106).

The self-evident phenomena of freewill is a boogey-bear to naturalists. It is obvious to the man on the street that freewill exists, that at any time he can choose to do otherwise *freely*. The reasons for believing in freewill are what philosphers would call intrinsic and irreducible (self-evident). If freewill is true (and it seems self-evidently to be so), it is outside of the scientific realm to explain and the door to metaphysics and religion is kicked wide open. The naturalist can't afford to do so. Freewill is possibly his thorniest problem.

Just as naturalists' presuppositions lead to a religion and the denial of freewill. Hard Calvinism accepts the philosophical presupposition of no freewill, then imposes that philosophy onto the Bible. Hard Calvinism is fatalism. It is philosophical determinism cloaked in the sheep's clothing of Bible language.

17. (See footnote 13 above also.) Peter says we are "elect according to foreknowledge." The hard Calvinist explains away the mystery suggesting that to be foreknown it has to be predetermined. As mentioned (see 13) such logic does not follow. In the *ordo saludis*, foreknowledge precedes election (see Rom 8:29). Even moderate Calvinists would say election and foreknowledge happen simultaneously with God, an Infinite who lives in an eternal "now." They would add that God doesn't think sequentially like we do. If He did, that implies that there is a time at which He wouldn't know everything, and that is impossible since God cannot change in His nature. Nevertheless the Bible affirms God's foreknowledge as logically prior to election. And we might add that it certainly *is* possible for God to think sequentially, but unlike us, such sequential thinking is instantaneous and intuitive, in God's perfect knowledge. In this regard, as so many other things dealing with the Infinite God, *exactly* how He thinks will have to remain a mystery to our finite minds—but not a contradiction.

18. God creates the *fact* of freedom; freewill creatures create the *acts* of freedom. Hyper-Calvinism, by the necessity of their position, have God causing the *acts* of humans—hardening them and so forth. God becomes the Author of sin, rather than freewill creatures.

Calvin taught that God made an eternal secret decree with Himself as to who would be saved and who would be reprobate. Humans had no freewill in the matter. That is a philosophical position which, once accepted, drives a theology that has come to be known as Reformed, or Dortian, or Five-Point Calvinism. At the synod of Dort were followers of Calvin who codified his system of thinking into five points, but actually went further than he did. For instance, it has been well-documented by R.T. Kendall and others that Calvin himself did not believe in limited atonement—the teaching that Christ died only for the elect. His thinking would lead there, and his followers took it there, but he himself did not believe in it. The five points are known by an acronym, TULIP. Total depravity, Unconditional election, Limited atonement, Irresistible grace, Perseverance of the saints.

In our opinion, virtually all of the points have serious Biblical problems when explained by hard-line Calvinists. Limited atonement, for instance, is certainly unbiblical on its face. "He Himself is the propitiation for our sins and not for our sins only, but for the sins of the *whole world*" (I Jn 2:2); "...we trust in the living God, who is the Savior of *all men*, especially of those who believe" (I Tim 4:10); even Calvin, explaining John 3:16 in his commentary, said "What can this mean but the *whole world* (whom Christ gave Himself for), not just the 'world of the elect'." The explanations that Calvinistic teachers use to explain away these and the many other passages teaching that Christ died for everyone and "whosoever will may come..." are so far-fetched as to be ridiculous. Though unbiblical, their position *is logical within their system*, that is to say, assuming their presuppositions (namely Calvin's primal assumption of God's secret, eternal decree with Himself...)

While we believe eternal security is not just part of the Gospel, it *is* the Gospel, the Calvinistic doctrine of perseverance has to be rejected because of its unbiblical nature. Namely there are commands to persevere; warnings if we fail to persevere; and the fact that not all

Christians *will* persevere, viz. Annanias and Saphira, King Saul, those who came unexamined to the Lord's table (I Cor 10:29-30); the sin unto death of a believer in I John 5:16-17 or James 5:19-20; the shipwreck of faith a believer could have in regard to not keeping a good conscience (I Tim 1:19-20); the straying from faith caused by greediness and false teaching (1 Tim 6:20-21), the possibility of disqualification if not operating by the rules (I Cor 9:27); and so forth. While eternal security is guaranteed, there is no guarantee about perseverance, only commands to do so and severe warnings if we don't.

Total depravity is Biblically dubious as well. Often Calvinists couch it that we are totally sinful apart from Christ, unable to do any good thing. Yet Jesus said, "How do you being evil give good gifts to your children?" We believe non-regenerate people can do good things, just not anything good enough to save themselves. Calvinists go much further. They are fond of associating total depravity with Romans 3:11, "There is none who seek after God." The fact is, God commands unsaved people to seek Him and has preappointed things in their lives to help cause it (Ac 17:26-27). There are several example in Acts and other places of unsaved people who sought the Lord, and God rewarded them for it (Cornelius, the Ethiopian eunuch, Apollos, the Nobleman in John 4, and others). Rather, what Romans 3:11 means is that *in and of ourselves* no one would seek after God. He must initiate it—and He has.

Having read Luther's *Bondage of the Will* my freshman year in college, I had toyed with the idea that we don't have freewill (It is fairly hard to live out. As Ryrie said, "Every Calvinist is an Arminian, i.e., believes in freewill, three times a day.") I finally rejected that notion my first year in seminary. Part of the reason was reading a poem by Charles Wesley to Andrew Toplady, a five-point Calvinist famous for writing *Rock of Ages Cleft For Me*. Notice his allusions to limited atonement, people not having freewill, and Calvin's eternal, secret "decree."

> A power to choose, a will to obey, freely His grace restores.
> All may find the Living Way and call the Savior ours.
>
> Horror to think that God is hate, fury in God could dwell.
> Could He a helpless world create to cast them into hell?

Down there an endless death to die
from which they could not flee?
No, Lord, Thine inmost bowles cry against the dire decree.

19.   Israel's *willful* unbelief is not mentioned but understood.   Any unbelieving Jew today feels no outside constraint or extrinsic force operating to keep him from belief. He would say that he is free to do and think as he does; there is no feeling of compulsion to not believe in Christ. He is free. Similarly, one must understand that all the rest of the Bible clearly teaches outright, or by implication, freewill. So why would it not be assumed here? To not see, that by figure of speech and only presenting one side of the equation (the Godward side), Paul wants to convey a specific feeling to the reader is to take an overly simplistic approach to the passage. God's sovereign election includes our freewill. Paul is free to speak only about one side of it for his purposes, his "authorial intent," but we are unwise, in light of the many other Scriptures, to assume there must *only be* one side.

For instance Paul says several times that he wants to move Israel to jealousy, but what would that matter if they are hardened by God from eternity and have no freewill as some insist? Paul—rather God since his words are God-breathed (2 Tim 3:16)—would simply be moving them to sin. God cannot be the Author of sin. Another reason he focuses only on the Godward side is, in the Gentiles case, to keep them humble (Rom 11:18, 22, 25).

20.   As Gary Brandenburg and others have noted, "There are none so blind as those who will not see."

21.   This is similar to our regeneration. Faith is logically prior to being saved, but chronologically it is at the same moment. There is no such thing as a saved person who does not believe, nor is there such a thing as a believer in Christ who is not saved. Faith and regeneration are simultaneous. The Bible says, "Believe and you shall be saved," not "Be saved and you shall believe." Calvinists, because of their understanding of total depravity, teach that regeneration precedes faith—a view that is most

certainly unbiblical. Faith is always the condition for eternal life. At the moment of faith regeneration has ocurred. "He who hears My words and believes Him who sent Me has eternal life, shall not come into condemnation, but has passed from death into life." Faith and regeneration must be simultaneous.

22. It can be said that God "hardened" Pharaoh's heart but it was *indirectly* and actually through His kindness and parience, a very different understanding than the hard-Calvinist construct. Solomon noticed, "Because the sentence against an evil work is not executed speedily, therefore the hearts of the sons of men is fully set in them to do evil" (Ecc 8:11). Because of God's patience in desiring us to repent, or in giving us further chances before executing His wrath, we might think we are getting away with something, or that there is nothing to fear from God. The more patient God is with us, the harder our hearts, the stiffer our necks, might become. God's forebearance and patience were intended on His side as a good thing; our evil hearts turned it into a "bad" thing (in that our hearts became more hardened). This seems the case with Pharaoh. Whatever the case, the Scripture record is not one of God simply zapping him and that he had no will in the matter.

23. The verb "to present" (yourselves to God) is an aorist infinitive, *parastēsai*. While it is unwise to make too much of a tense, that Paul uses an aorist rather than a present tense *could* imply a one-time kind of act. Many Christians have testified to such an experience, being able to recall a time, or point in their lives, where they made a once-for-all kind of commitment of their lives to the Lord. Rather than the *daily* presenting ourselves to the Lord which we should all do (Lk 9:23), this might refer to that *moment* where we turn the reigns over to God *for good* (at least that being our sincere intention). But even if we don't, we're still in the family!

24. Anytime someone suggests there are "steps" involved in the Gospel, "1-2-3's," or "A,B,C's," you better have red lights going off in your head. Immediately after the Lord gave the Ten Commandments (Ex 20:1-23), He gave instructions about the sacrificial altar. No wonder, since we

185

certainly weren't able to keep His Law! The altar speaks to us of Christ and His substitutionary death, in particular to the Gospel which holds that message. The Lord says no human "tool" was to be used upon the altar (20:25), "Nor shall you go up by steps to My altar, lest your nakedness be exposed" (20:26). If we put a "tool" on, or make "steps" to the altar, we have "profaned" it, He says. We've put our finger prints on it, so to speak. Remember that God has chosen the message of the cross to save us, in part so that "no flesh should glory in His presence… that just as it is written, 'Let him who glories, glory in the Lord'" (I Co 1:29, 31). The glory of the Gospel is reserved for Christ alone. We can't brag about it or claim to have had a part in it.

The Gospel has no "steps." One either believes it or he doesn't. "Most assuredly I say to you, whoever believes in Me has eternal life." It's not "Believe and ____," or "Do this and this *and* believe…." It's believe, period. *No steps!* When we make "steps" to the "altar"—to the Gospel— inevitably it will come down to something other than simple belief, and usually some kind of work, explicit or implicit, is introduced. Then it's of works and not of grace, which cannot be (Ro 11:6[!]). Further, it gives ground for boasting.

I saw this speaker's "nakedness" exposed (who made steps in the Gospel) the next day. There was a Questions Seminar. Several wrote the same question, "How can I know for sure I'm going to heaven?" I watched him squirm trying to answer their honest questions, but he couldn't. His theology gives no objective assurance since works are involved implicitly.

In front of them, he deferred the question to me. How happy I was for an opportunity to simply say, "*Assurance* is part and parcel of Christ's very words when He says, '*Most assuredly*, I say to you, whoever believes in Me has eternal life.' If you believe Him for that promise—*believe Him* that all you have to do is *believe Him* for eternal life—then you know you have eternal life. If you don't *know* you have eternal life, then you are not believing Him. It is that simple." With deepest emotion now as I review it in my mind, ten years ago now, I remember on those few words the kids smiling and resting easy as they perceived the joyful assurance of such a simple promise.

For information about ordering more books,
or for group pricing, please contact:

Allie Grace Publishers
972-686-0065
or email us at
steveandmarcielkins@msn.com

If this book has been a blessing to you and you would like to make a
donation to the urban ministry of East Dallas Young Life, you can
make your check payable and mail it to:

East Dallas Young Life
9706 La Prada
Dallas, Texas 75228

Your gift is appreciated and tax-deductible